Best of

SCANDINAVIA

*Make the Most of Every Day
and Every Dollar*

**John Muir Publications
Santa Fe, New Mexico**

Originally published as *22 Days in Norway, Sweden, and Denmark*

Other JMP travel guidebooks by Rick Steves
Asia Through the Back Door (with Bob Effertz)
Europe 101: History, Art, and Culture for the Traveler
    (with Gene Openshaw)
Mona Winks: Self-Guided Tours of Europe's Top Museums
    (with Gene Openshaw)
Rick Steves' Best of the Baltics and Russia (with Ian Watson)
Rick Steves' Best of Europe
Rick Steves' Best of France, Belgium, and the Netherlands
    (with Steve Smith)
Rick Steves' Best of Germany, Austria, and Switzerland
Rick Steves' Best of Great Britain
Rick Steves' Best of Italy
Rick Steves' Best of Spain and Portugal
Rick Steves' Europe Through the Back Door
Rick Steves' Phrase Books: French, German, Italian,
    Spanish and Portuguese, and French/German/Italian

John Muir Publications, P.O. Box 613, Santa Fe, NM 87504

© 1995 by Rick Steves
Cover © 1995 by John Muir Publications
All rights reserved
Printed in the United States of America
First printing, January 1995

ISSN 1078-8042
ISBN 1-56261-200-X

Editor Risa Laib
Editorial Support Elizabeth Wolf, Jean Teeters, Dianna
  Delling
Production Kathryn Lloyd-Strongin, Sarah Johansson
Maps David C. Hoerlein
Cover Design Tony D'Agostino

Interior Design Linda Braun
Typesetting Cowgirls Design, Taos, New Mexico
Printer Banta Company
Cover photo Leo de Wys, Inc. /Geoffrey Hiller

Distributed to the book trade by
Publishers Group West
Emeryville, California

Thanks to Dave Hoerlein and my wife, Anne, for research help
and support. Thanks also to Thor, Berit, Hanne, Geir, Hege
and Kari-Anne, our Norwegian family.

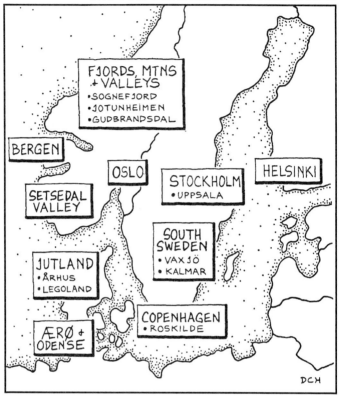

CONTENTS

HOW TO USE THIS BOOK

This book breaks Scandinavia into its top 11 big city, small town, and rural destinations. It then gives you all the information and opinions necessary to wring the maximum value out of your limited time and money in each of these destinations.

If you plan a month or less in Scandinavia, and have a normal appetite for information, this lean and mean little book is all you need.

Experiencing the culture, people, and natural wonders of Scandinavia economically and hassle-free has been my goal for 20 years of traveling, tour guiding, and travel writing. With this book, I pass on to you the lessons I've learned, updated for 1995.

Rick Steves' Best of Scandinavia is your smiling Swede, your Nordic navigator, a tour guide in your pocket. This book is balanced to include a comfortable mix of exciting capital cities and cozy small towns. It covers the predictable biggies and mixes in a healthy dose of Back Door intimacy. Along with Tivoli Gardens, Hans Christian Andersen's house, and the Little Mermaid, you'll take a bike tour of a sleepy remote Danish isle, dock at a time-passed fjord village, and wander among eerie, prehistoric monoliths in Sweden. To save time, maximize diversity, and avoid tourist burn-out, I've been very selective. We won't cruise both the Geirangerfjord and the Sognefjord, just the better of the two.

I don't recommend anything just to fill a hole. If you find no tips on eating in a town, I've yet to find a restaurant worth recommending over the others. In the interest of smart use of your time, I favor hotels and restaurants handy to your sightseeing activities and public transportation. Rather than list hotels scattered throughout a city, I choose a convenient and colorful neighborhood and recommend its best accommodations values, from $10 bunk beds to $140 doubles.

The best is, of course, only my opinion. But after two busy decades of travel writing, lecturing, and tour guiding, I've developed a sixth sense of what tickles the traveler's fancy.

This Information Is Accurate and Up-to-Date

This book is up-dated every year. Most publishers of guide-books that cover a country from top to bottom can afford an update only every two or three years (and even then, it's often by letter). Since this book is selective, covering only the places I think make the top month or so in each country, I'm able to personally update it each year. Even with an annual update, things change. But if you're traveling with the current edition of this book, I guarantee you're using the most up-to-date information available. If you're packing an old book, you'll learn the seriousness of your mistake by day two. (Your trip costs about $10 per waking hour. Your time is valuable. This guidebook saves lots of time.)

2 to 22 Days Out . . . Modularity In! Scandinavia's Top 10 Destinations

This book used to be called *2 to 22 Days in Norway, Sweden, and Denmark*. It was organized as a proposed 22-day route. It's now restructured into a more flexible modular system. Each recommended module, or destination, is covered as a mini-vacation on its own, filled with exciting sights, homey affordable places to stay, and hard opinions on how to best use your limited time. As before, my assumption is that you have limited time and money. My goal remains to help you get the most travel experience out of each day and each dollar. Each destination is broken into these sections:

Planning Your Time, a suggested schedule with thoughts on how to best use your time.

Orientation, including transportation within a destination, tourist information, and a DCH map designed to make the text clear and your entry smooth.

Sights with ratings: ▲▲▲—Don't miss; ▲▲—Try hard to see; ▲—Worthwhile if you can make it; No rating—Worth knowing about.

Sleeping and **Eating**, with addresses and phone numbers of my favorite budget hotels and restaurants.

Transportation Connections to nearby destinations by train and Route Tips for Drivers, with ideas on road-side attractions along the way.

The **Appendix** is a traveler's tool kit with information on climate, telephone numbers, and public transportation.

Browse through this book, choose your favorite destinations, link them up, and have a great trip. You'll travel like a temporary local, getting the absolute most out of every mile, minute, and kroner. You won't waste time on mediocre sights because, unlike other guidebooks, I cover only my favorites. Since a major financial pitfall is expensive hotels, I've worked hard to assemble the best accommodations values for each stop. And as you travel, I'm happy you'll be meeting some of my favorite Scandinavian people.

Costs

Five components make up the cost of your trip: airfare, surface transportation, room and board, sightseeing, and shopping/entertainment/miscellaneous.

Airfare: Don't try to sort through the mess. Get and use a good travel agent. A basic round-trip U.S.A. to Copenhagen flight should cost $600-$1,000, depending on where you fly from and when. Consider "open-jaws."

Surface Transportation: For a 3-week whirlwind trip of all my recommended destinations, allow $500 per person for public transportation (first class, 21-day Scanrail pass and extra boat rides, $400, second class), or $600 per person (based on two people sharing car and gas) for a 3-week car rental, tolls, gas, and insurance.

Room and Board: In 1995, you can eat and sleep well in Scandinavia for $60 a day plus transportation costs. Students and tightwads will do it on $40. A $60-a-day budget allows $35 for a double with breakfast, $10 for lunch, and $15 for dinner. That's basic and alcohol-free, but doable. Budget sleeping and eating requires the skills and information covered in this book.

Sightseeing: In big cities, figure $5-$10 per major sight, $2 for minor ones, and $25 for splurge experiences (e.g., tours or folk concerts). The capital cities each have cards giving you a 24-hour free run of the public transit system and entrance to all the sights for about $20. An overall average of $15 a day works for most people. Don't skimp here. After all, this category directly powers most of the experiences all the other expenses are designed to make possible.

Shopping/Entertainment/Miscellaneous: In Scandinavia, this category can brutalize your budget.

While Scandinavia is expensive, transportation passes, groceries, alternative accommodations, admissions, and enjoying nature are affordable (about what you'd pay in England or Italy). When things are expensive, remind yourself you're not getting less for your travel dollar. Up here, there simply aren't any lousy or cheap alternatives to classy, cozy, sleek Scandinavia. Electronic eyes flush youth hostel toilets and breakfasts are all-you-can-eat.

If you take full advantage of this book, it will save you a ship-load of money and days of headaches. Read it carefully from start to finish. Many of the general skills and cheap tricks used in Copenhagen work in Oslo and Stockholm as well.

Prices and Discounts

To figure approximate prices in this book: 7 kroner = $1. I've priced things in local currencies throughout the book. While each of the Scandinavian countries' kroner have different values, they are close. All kroner are decimalized— 100 ore equals 1 krone. The money is not accepted outside of its home turf (except, of course, at foreign exchange services and banks). Standard abbreviations are: Danish krone, DKK; Swedish krone, SEK; and Norwegian krone, NOK. We'll keep it simple and use the krone abbreviation, kr, for Denmark, Sweden, and Norway. To translate local prices into U.S. dollars, divide by 7 (35 kr = about $5). The Finnish markka (FIM or mk) is worth about 20 cents (5 mk = about $1).

I have not listed discounts in this book. But in keeping with its social orientation, Scandinavia is Europe's most generous corner when it comes to youth, student, senior, and family discounts. If you are any of the above, always mention it. Students should travel with the ISIC card (normally available at University Foreign Study offices). Spouses often pay half price when doing things as a couple. Children usually pay half price or less (for example, in hostels).

Sample Itineraries
Priority of Nordic Sightseeing Stops

3 days:	Copenhagen, Stockholm, Oslo connected by night trains
5 days, add:	More time in capitals
7 days, add:	"Norway in a Nutshell" fjord trip, Bergen
10 days, add:	6-hour cruise to Helsinki, and slow down
14 days, add:	Aero, Odense, Roskilde, Frederiksborg
17 days, add:	Jutland, Kalmar
21 days, add:	Lillehammer, Jotenheim, Vaxjo, Setesdal
24 days, add:	Riga and Tallinn
30 days, add:	Side trip to St Petersburg, and slow down

Whirlwind Three-Week Tour

(The map and suggested three-week itinerary on previous page include everything in the top 21 days.)

Scandinavia's Best 21-Day Trip

Days	Plan	Sleep in
1	Arrive in Copenhagen	Copenhagen
2	Copenhagen	Copenhagen
3	Copenhagen	Copenhagen
4	North Zealand, into Sweden	Vaxjo
5	Vaxjo, Kalmar, Glass Country	Kalmar
6	Kalmar to Stockholm	Stockhol
7	Stockholm	Stockholm
8	Stockholm	boat
9	Helsinki	boat
10	Uppsala to Oslo	Oslo
11	Oslo	Oslo
12	Oslo	Oslo
13	Lillehammer, Gudbrandsdalen	Jotenheim/ Sogndal
14	Jotenheim Country	Sogndal/ Aurland
15	Sognefjord, Norway in Nutshell	Bergen
16	Bergen	Bergen
17	Long drive south, Setesdal	boat
18	Jutland, Arhus, Legoland	Arhus/Billund
19	Jutland to Aero	Aeroskobing
20	Aero	Aeroskobing

While this three-week itinerary is designed to be done by car, it can be done by train and bus. Scandinavia in 21 days by train is most efficient with a little reworking: I'd go overnight whenever possible on any train ride 6 or more hours long. Streamline by doing North Zealand, Odense, and Aero as a 3-day side trip from Copenhagen, skipping the Vaxjo-Kalmar day, and spending the night on the very efficient Copenhagen-Stockholm train (there is no Copenhagen-Kalmar overnight train). The Bergen/Setesdal/Arhus/Copenhagen leg is possible on public transit, but getting from Bergen to Kristiansand will test your patience, and Setesdal is not worth the trouble if you don't have the poke-around freedom a car gives you. If you really want to see Legos and the Bogman, do Jutland from Copenhagen. A flight straight home from Bergen is wonderfully efficient. Otherwise, it's about 20 hours by train from Bergen to Copenhagen via Oslo.

When to Go

Summer is by far the best. Scandinavia bustles and glistens under the July and August sun. Scandinavian schools get out around June 20, most local industries take July off, and the British and central Europeans tend to visit Scandinavia in August. You'll notice crowds during these times, but it's never as crowded as southern Europe. While you could do the trip with no hotel reservations, I compare prices and get my favorite places by calling a day or two in advance as I go. (I update this book each July.)

"Shoulder season" travel (in late May, early June, and September), with minimal crowds, decent weather, and sights and tourist fun spots still open, lacks the vitality of summer. Things quiet down when the local kids go back to school (around August 20).

°Winter has no tourist crowds for good reason. It's a bad time to explore Scandinavia. Many sights and accommodations are closed or open on a limited schedule. Business travelers drive hotel prices way up. Winter weather can be cold and dreary, and nighttime will draw the shades on your sightseeing well before dinner.

Travel Smart

When you arrive in a town, make arrangements for your departure. Use the telephone for reservations and confirmations, and visit local tourist information offices. Ask questions. Most locals are eager to point you in their idea of the right direction. Carry a phone card, wear a money belt, organize your thoughts and plans on paper, and practice the virtue of simplicity. If you insist on being confused, your trip will be a mess. Those who expect to travel smart, do.

Tourist Information

Any town with much tourism has a well-organized, English-speaking tourist information office (which I'll call "TI"). The TI should be your first stop in a new city. Try to arrive, or at least telephone, before they close.

While the TIs have a room-finding service, these are a good deal only if you're in search of summer and weekend deals on business hotels. They can help you with small pensions and private homes, but you'll save both you and your host money by going direct with the listings in this book.

The Scandinavian National Tourist Office in the U.S.A. is a wealth of information (655 3rd Ave., 18th Floor, New York, NY 10017, 212/949-2333, fax 212/983-5260). Before your trip, get their free general information booklet covering all five countries and request any specific information you may want (city maps, calendars of events, and specifics).

Recommended Guidebooks

If you'll be traveling beyond my recommended destinations, you may want some supplemental information. When you consider the improvements they'll make in your $3,000 vacation, $25 or $35 for extra maps and books is money well spent. Especially for several people traveling by car, the weight and expense are negligible.

The Lonely Planet Guide to Scandinavia is thorough, well researched, and packed with good maps and hotel recommendations for low-to-moderate budget travelers. The hip *Rough Guide* to Scandinavia is thick. *Let's Go* only has skimpy chapters on Scandinavia in its Europe edition. Because of the relatively small market, there just aren't many guidebooks out on Scandinavia. I think of all my "best of" country guidebooks, this one fills the biggest void.

Rick Steves' Books

Rick Steves' Europe Through the Back Door, 13th Edition (Santa Fe, NM: John Muir Publications, 1995) gives you budget travel skills such as minimizing jet lag, packing light, driving or train travel, finding budget beds without reservations, changing money, theft, terrorism, hurdling the language barrier, health, travel photography, what to do with your bidet, ugly-

Americanism, laundry, itinerary strategies, and more.
The book also includes chapters on my forty favorite
"Back Doors."

Rick Steves' Country Guides are a series of eight
guidebooks covering the Baltics and Russia, Europe, France,
Germany/Austria/Switzerland, Great Britain, Italy, and
Spain/Portugal, in the way this one covers Scandinavia.

Europe 101: History and Art for the Traveler (co-written
with Gene Openshaw, John Muir Publications, 1990) gives
you the story of Europe's people, history, and art (but,
like most European histories, it has little to say about
Scandinavia). A little "101" background knowledge really
helps Europe's sights come alive. Likewise, my *Mona Winks*
(John Muir Publications, 1993, also co-written with Gene
Openshaw), gives you fun, easy-to-follow self-guided tours of
Europe's top 20 museums, but nothing on Scandinavia.

While I've designed a series of four phrase books, there
is virtually no language barrier in Scandinavia, so I wouldn't
bother with a phrase book for traveling here.

Maps
While train travelers can fake it with freebie maps, drivers
should get one good overall road map for Scandinavia (either
the Michelin Scandinavia or the Kummerly and Frey
Southern Scandinavia 1:1,000,000 edition). The only detailed
map worth considering is the "Southern Norway-North"
(Sor Norge-nord, 1:325,000) by Cappelens Kart ($12 in
Scandinavian bookstores). Excellent city and regional maps
are available from local TIs, usually for free.

The maps in this book, drawn by Dave Hoerlein,
are concise and simple. Dave, who is well-traveled in
Scandinavia, has designed the maps to help you locate recommended places and the tourist offices, where you'll find
more in-depth maps of the necessary cities or regions.

Getting to Scandinavia
Copenhagen is the most direct and least expensive Scandi-
navian capital to fly into from the U.S.A. Copenhagen is also
Europe's gateway to Scandinavia from points south. There
are often cheaper flights from the U.S.A. into Frankfurt and
Amsterdam than into Copenhagen. It's a long, rather dull,

one-day drive to Scandinavia from Amsterdam or Frankfurt (with a 2-hour, $60 per car and passenger ferry crossing at Puttgarten). By train, the trip is effortless—overnight from Amsterdam or Frankfurt. The $120 trip is included with your Eurailpass (but not the Scanrail pass).

Transportation in Scandinavia

By Car or Train?

While a car gives you the ultimate in mobility and freedom, enables you to search for hotels more easily, and carries your bags for you, the train zips you effortlessly from city to city, usually dropping you in the center and near the tourist office. Cars are great in the countryside, but an expensive headache in places like Oslo, Copenhagen, and Bergen. Three or four travel cheaper by car. With a few exceptions, trains cover my recommended destinations wonderfully. And the Scanrail pass is one of the great Nordic bargains.

There are two Scanrail passes (each with several variations): one sold in the U.S.A. and one in Scandinavia. The one sold in Scandinavia is purchased easily on the spot at any major train station. Both give you free run of all trains in the region and many boats (such as Stockholm to Finland). Both passes go easy on the mark up for first class. Even though Scandinavian second class is like southern European first class, for $5 a day extra, you might consider first class. Scanrail 'n' Drive passes offer a flexible and economical way to mix rail and car rental (which comes in handy if you're planning to explore the Norwegian mountains and fjords). A Eurailpass, which costs much more than a comparable Scanrail pass, is a good value only for those coming to Scandinavia from central Europe (a 3-week first-class Eurailpass costs about $650).

If traveling by train, remember the efficiency of night travel. The couchette supplement (a bed in a compartment with two triple bunks) costs $15 beyond your first or second class ticket or pass. A "sleeper," giving you the privacy of a double or triple compartment, costs about $30. Reservations are required on the super-fast Danish and Swedish trains and on all long Norwegian trips.

Cost of Public Transportation

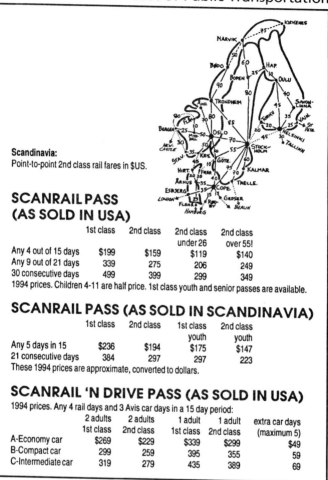

Scandinavia:
Point-to-point 2nd class rail fares in $US.

SCANRAIL PASS
(AS SOLD IN USA)

	1st class	2nd class	2nd class under 26	2nd class over 55!
Any 4 out of 15 days	$199	$159	$119	$140
Any 9 out of 21 days	339	275	206	249
30 consecutive days	499	399	299	349

1994 prices. Children 4-11 are half price. 1st class youth and senior passes are available.

SCANRAIL PASS (AS SOLD IN SCANDINAVIA)

	1st class	2nd class	1st class youth	2nd class youth
Any 5 days in 15	$236	$194	$175	$147
21 consecutive days	384	297	297	223

These 1994 prices are approximate, converted to dollars.

SCANRAIL 'N DRIVE PASS (AS SOLD IN USA)

1994 prices. Any 4 rail days and 3 Avis car days in a 15 day period:

	2 adults 1st class	2 adults 2nd class	1 adult 1st class	1 adult 2nd class	extra car days (maximum 5)
A-Economy car	$269	$229	$339	$299	$49
B-Compact car	299	259	395	355	59
C-Intermediate car	319	279	435	389	69

Car Rental

Car rental is usually cheapest when arranged (well in advance) in the United States through your travel agent, rather than in Scandinavia. You'll want a weekly rate with unlimited mileage. If you're traveling for more than three weeks, ask your agent about leasing a car. Each major car rental agency has an office in the Copenhagen airport. Comparison shop through your agent and Rafco (see below).

Rafco, a small Danish company near Copenhagen (associated with Thrifty), rents nearly-new Peugeots at almost trouble-making prices. The manager, Ken, promises my readers a 10 percent discount over his already thrifty prices. For example, he'll give 10 percent off the "money saver" rate (including taxes, free mileage, and airport delivery) for a Group A car (like a Peugeot 106) of 194 kr, plus 31 kr for CDW (about $35) a day (minimum 21 days). Similar rates apply on automatics, station wagons, mini-buses, and other models. They also have new, small motor homes that are very popular for families on a budget (about $750 a week, with gear, 4-6 beds, kitchen, WC, and a 10% discount to this book's readers). For more information and their brochure, call or write to Rafco: Englandsvej 380, DK-2770 Kastrup, Denmark, tel. 45/31 51 15 00, fax 45/31 51 10 89. By the way, Rafco often needs drivers to deliver or return cars between Copenhagen and Paris or Amsterdam. Call for the possibility of a free trip.

Driving in Scandinavia

Except for the dangers posed by the scenic distractions and moose crossings, Scandinavia is a great place to drive. Your American license is accepted. Gas is expensive, over $4 per gallon (gas in Denmark is substantially cheaper than its northern neighbors), roads are good (but nerve-rackingly skinny in western Norway), traffic is generally sparse, drivers are sober and civil, signs and road maps are excellent, local road etiquette is similar to the U.S., and seat belts are required. Use your headlights day and night; it's required in most of Scandinavia. Bikes whiz by close and quiet, so be on guard.

There are plenty of good facilities, gas stations, and scenic rest stops. Snow is a serious problem off-season in the mountains. Parking is a headache only in major cities, where expensive garages are safe and plentiful. Denmark uses a parking windshield clock disk (free; set it when you arrive and be back before your posted time limit is up). Even in the Nordic countries, thieves break into cars. Park carefully, use the trunk, and show no valuables. Never drink and drive. Even one drink can get a driver into serious trouble.

As you navigate, you'll find town signs followed by the letters n, s, o, v, or c. These stand for north, south, east, west, and center, respectively, and understanding them will save you lots of wrong exits. Due to recent changes, many maps have the wrong road numbers. It's safest to navigate by town names.

Sleeping in Scandinavia

Accommodations expenses will make or break your budget. Vagabonds sleep happily everywhere for $15. An overall average of $60 per night per double is possible using this book's listings. Unless otherwise noted, the accommodations I've listed will hold a room with a phone call until 18:00 with no deposit, and the proprietors speak English. I like places that are small, central, clean, traditional, friendly, and not listed in other guidebooks. Most places listed meet five of these six virtues.

Tourist Office room-finding services, if you have no place in mind, can be worth the 30 kr fee. Be very clear about what you want. (Say "cheap," and whether you have sheets or a sleeping bag, will take a twin or double, don't require a shower, and so on.) They know the hotel quirks and private-room scene better than anybody. Official price listings are often misleading, since they omit cheaper oddball rooms and special clearance deals.

To sleep cheap, bring your own sheet or sleeping bag and offer to provide it in low-priced establishments. This can save $10 per person per night, especially in rural areas. Families can get a price break; normally a child can sleep very cheap in mom and dad's room. To get the most sleep for your dollar, pull the dark shades to keep out the very early morning sun.

The Sleep Code

To save space while giving more specific information for people with special concerns, I've described my recommended hotels with a standard code. When there is a range of prices in one category, the price will fluctuate with the season, size of room, or length of stay.

S—Single room or price for one person using a double.

D—Double or twin room. Double beds are usually big enough for non-romantic couples.

T—Three-person room (often a double bed with a single bed moved in).

Q—Four-adult room (an extra child's bed is usually cheaper).

B—Private shower (most likely) or bath in the room. Most B rooms have a WC (toilet). All rooms have a sink. B rooms are often bigger and renovated while the cheaper rooms without B often will be on the top floor or yet to be refurbished. Any room without B has access to a B on the corridor (free unless otherwise noted). Rooms with baths often cost more than rooms with showers.

WC—I include this only to differentiate between rooms that have only a B and those with BWC. With no WC mentioned, B rooms generally have a WC.

CC—Accepts credit cards: V=Visa, M=Mastercard, A= American Express. Many also accept Diners (which I ignored). If CC is not mentioned, assume they accept only cash.

Hotels

Hotels are expensive ($80-$150 doubles) with some exceptions. Business-class hotels dump prices to attract tourists with "summer" and "weekend" rates (Friday, Saturday, and sometimes Sunday). The much-advertised hotel discount cards or clubs offer nothing more than these rates which are open to everyone anyway. To sleep in a fancy hotel, it's cheapest to arrive without a reservation and let the local tourist office book you a room. Hotels are expensive, but when a classy, modern $200 place has a $100 summer special that includes two $10 buffet breakfasts, the dumpy $60 hotel room without breakfast becomes less exciting.

There are actually several tiers of rates including: tourist office, weekend, summer, summer weekend, and walk in. "Walk ins" at the end of a quiet day can often get a room even below the summer rate. Many modern hotels have "combi" rooms (singles with a sofa that makes into a perfectly good double) which are cheaper than a full double. Also, many places have low-grade older rooms, considered unacceptable for the general public and often used by workers on weekdays outside of summer. If you're on a budget, ask for cheaper rooms with no windows or no water. And if a hotel is not full, any day can become a summer day.

Hostels

Scandinavian hostels, Europe's finest, are open to travelers of all ages. They offer classy facilities, members' kitchens, cheap hot meals, plenty of doubles (for a few extra kroner), and great people experiences. Receptionists speak English and will hold a room if you promise to arrive by 18:00. Many close in the off-season. Buy a membership card before you leave home. Those without cards are admitted for a $5 per night guest membership fee. Bring bedsheets from home or plan on renting them for about $5 a night. You'll find lots of Volvos in hostel parking lots, as Scandinavians know hostels provide the best (and usually only) $15 beds in town. Hosteling is ideal for the two-bunk family (4-bed rooms, kitchens, washing machines, discount family memberships). Pick up each country's free hostel directory at any hostel or TI.

Camping

Scandinavian campgrounds are practical, comfortable, and cheap ($5 per person with camping card, available on the spot). The national tourist office has a fine brochure/map listing all their campgrounds. This is the middle-class Scandinavian family way to travel: safe, great social fun, and no reservation problems.

Huts

Most campgrounds provide huts (Hytter) for wannabe campers with no gear. Huts normally sleep 4-6 in bunk beds, come with blankets, a kitchenette, and charge one fee (around $40), plus extra if you need sheets. Since locals typically move in for a week or two, many campground huts are booked for summer long in advance. If you're driving late, with no place to stay, find a campground and grab a hut.

Private Rooms

Throughout Scandinavia, people rent out rooms in their homes to travelers for around $40 per double. Prices are so cheap because it's a "taxation optional" form of income in Europe's most highly taxed corner. While some put out a Rom, Rum, or Hus Rum sign, most operate solely through the local tourist office (which occasionally keeps these B&B a secret until all hotel rooms are taken). You'll get your own key to a lived-in, clean, and comfortable (but usually simple) private room with free access to the family shower and WC. Booking direct saves both you and your host the cut the tourist office takes. (The tourist offices are very protective of their lists. If you enjoy a big city private home that would like to be listed in this book, I'd love to hear from you.)

Reservations

Unless you have a particular place you really want to stay in (such as a B&B or one of the fancy mountain hotels I recommend) do this trip making reservations a day in advance as you travel. If you'd be more comfortable with firm reservations, they're easy by telephone. You can book your entire trip by phone from home in about an hour for around $50. If you'll be arriving early, ask if you can simply reconfirm by telephone a day or two in advance (rather than sending a deposit). It doesn't hurt to mention this book. Keep track of reservations made. It's no problem to cancel. But it's a big problem if you just don't show up. Please! I've promised my hotel friends that my readers are more reliable than the average American traveler in this regard. In return, most of them agree to hold a room with no deposit until at least late afternoon of the day you'll arrive. (If you need to arrive very late, "plan" to arrive early and reassure them with phone calls the day of your late arrival.) Not having to send deposits makes your trip simpler and more flexible.

Eating in Scandinavia

The smartest budget travelers do as the Scandinavians do— avoid restaurants. Prepared food is heavily taxed, and the local cuisine just isn't worth trip bankruptcy. Of course, you'll want to take an occasional splurge into each culture's high cuisine, but the "high" refers mostly to the price tag. Why not think of eating on the road as eating at home without your kitchen? Get creative with cold food and picnics. I eat well on a budget in Scandinavia with the following approach.

Breakfast

Hotel breakfasts are a huge and filling buffet, normally an $8-$10 option. This includes cereal or porridge, *let* (lowfat) or *sod* (whole) milk, or various kinds of drinkable yogurt (pour the yogurt in the bowl and sprinkle the crispy cereal over it), bread, crackers, cheese (the brown stuff is goat's cheese and your trip will go much better when you develop a taste for it); cold cuts, and jam; fruit; juice and coffee, or tea. Coffee addicts can buy a thermos and get it filled in most hotels and hostels for $3 or $4.

I bring a baggie to breakfast and leave with a light lunch—sandwich and apple or a can of yogurt. Yes, I know, this is almost stealing, but here's how I rationalize it: Throughout my trip, I'm paying lots of taxes to support a social system that my host (but not me) will enjoy; I could have eaten what I take at that all-you-can-eat sitting, but choose to finish breakfast elsewhere . . . later. And the Vikings did much worse things. After a big breakfast, a light baggie lunch fits nicely into a busy sightseeing day.

If you skip your hotel's breakfast, you can visit a bakery to get a sandwich and cup of coffee. Bakeries have wonderful inexpensive pastries. The only cheap breakfast is one you make yourself. Many simple accommodations provide kitchenettes, or at least hot pads and coffee pots.

Lunch

Scandinavians aren't big on lunch, often just grabbing a sandwich (*smorrebrod*) and a cup of coffee at their work desk. Follow suit with a quick picnic or a light meal at a sandwich shop or snack bar.

Picnics

Scandinavia has colorful markets and economical supermarkets. Picnic-friendly mini-markets at gas and train stations are open late. Some shopping tips: Wasa cracker bread (Sport is my favorite, Ideal flatbrod is ideal for munchies), prepackaged meat and cheese, goat cheese (*geitost*; *ekte* means pure and stronger), yogurt (you can drink it out of the carton), freshly cooked fish in markets, fresh fruit and vegetables, lingonberries, mustard and sandwich spreads (shrimp, caviar) in a squeeze tube, boxes of juice, milk, *pytt i panna* (Swedish hash), and rye bread (look for "rag," sweet as cake). Grocery stores sell a cheap, light breakfast: a handy yogurt with cereal and a spoon. If you're lazy, most places offer cheap ready-made sandwiches. If you're bored, most places have hot chicken, salads by the portion, fresh and cheap liver pâté, and other ways to picnic without sandwiches.

Dinner

The large meal of the Nordic day is an early dinner. Alternate between cheap, forgettable, but filling, cafeteria or fast food dinners ($12), and atmospheric, carefully chosen restaurants popular with locals ($20). Look for the "*dagens ratt,*" an affordable one-plate daily special. One main course and two salads or soups fills up two travelers without emptying their pocketbooks. The cheap eateries close early, because in Scandinavia a normal, practical, fill-the-tank dinner is usually eaten around 18:00. Anyone eating out later is "dining," will linger longer, and expect to pay much more. A $15 Scandinavian meal is not that much more than a $10 American meal, since tax and tip are included in the menu price.

In most Scandinavian restaurants, you can ask for more potatoes or vegetables, so a restaurant entrée is basically an all-you-can-eat deal. First servings are often small so take advantage of this. Fast food joints, pizzerias, Chinese food, and salad bars are inexpensive. Booze will break you. Drink water (served free with an understanding smile at any restaurant). Waitresses are well paid and tips are normally included, although it's polite to round up the bill.

Most nations have one inedible dish that is cherished with a perverse but patriotic sentimentality. These dishes often originate with a famine and are kept in use to remind the young of their foremothers' and forefathers' suffering. Norway's penitential food, lutefisk (dried cod marinated for several days in potash and water), is used for Christmas and jokes.

The Language Barrier

Of course, it would be great to speak the local language, but in Scandinavia, English is all you need. They say a Scandinavian can speak any language that will separate a tourist from his money. Whatever the motive, especially among the young, English is Scandinavia's foreign language of choice. In fact, English is well on its way to doing to the Scandinavian languages what it did to the old Irish. Learn the polite words and a few very basic phrases and you'll have absolutely no problems.

A few words you'll see a lot are: *gamla* (old), *stor* (big), *takk* (thanks), *slot* (castle or palace), *fart* (trip, comes in many varieties), *time* (hour), *centrum* (center), *ikke* (no, not, as in "don't do it"), and *salg* (sale).

Even though these days small children watch and understand cartoons in English, each country does have its own distinct language. Except for Finnish, they are closely related and have many similarities to English (a cousin of the Nordic tongues). The Scandinavians have several letters (Æ, Å, Ø) that we don't have. To keep things simple in this book, I have opted to spell Scandinavian words with only our letters. This really blows the pronunciation for those who speak these languages. But for most of us, the only problem this causes is in alphabetizing. Whenever I can't find something (such as the word for the town "Århus" in the map index), I look after "Z" where they store the special letters of the Nordic alphabet. My apologies to these languages for my laziness.

One Region, Different Countries

Scandinavia is western Europe's least populated, most literate, most prosperous, most demographically homogenous, least church-going, most highly taxed, and most socialistic corner.

While Finland and Iceland are odd ducks in northern Europe, Denmark, Norway, and Sweden are pretty similar. They each have distinct but closely related languages (so close that they can laugh at each other's TV comedies). While the state religion is Lutheran and 90 percent of the people are registered as Lutherans, only a small percentage actually go to church outside of Easter or Christmas.

Each country is a constitutional monarchy with a royal family that knows how to stay out of the tabloids and work with the parliaments. Scandinavia is the home of cradle-to-grave security and, consequently, the most highly taxed corner of Europe. Schools must be good, because illiteracy is nearly unknown and almost everybody speaks English. Blessed with a pristine nature and sparse populations, the Scandinavians are environmentalists (except for the Norwegian appetite for whaling). The region is also a leader in progressive lifestyles and social experiments. Over half the young married couples in Denmark are only "married" because they've lived together for so long and have children.

Denmark, packing 5 million fun-loving Danes into a flat and gentle land the size of Switzerland, is the most densely populated. Sweden, the size of California, has 8.5 million (mostly blondes). And 4.2 million Norwegians stretch out in long and skinny Norway. (It's as far from Oslo to the north tip of Norway as it is from Oslo to Rome.)

Each country is super-well organized. Each uses a krown for its currency (all different but worth about the same: 7 = $1).

Red Tape and Banking

Traveling throughout this region requires only a passport—no shots and no visas. Border crossings between Norway, Sweden, Denmark, and Finland are a wave through. When you change countries, however, you do change money, postage stamps, and more. Local sales taxes are refunded at the border for souvenirs and gifts purchased. Ask local merchants for instructions.

Banking in Scandinavia is straightforward. You'll have almost no loss because of the buy and sell rates (they're within about 2% of each other). Exchange rates are nearly standard. The banks make their money off a stiff 10 kr-30 kr per check fee (normally with a 20 kr or 30 kr minimum). Bring traveler's checks in big denominations. If you have only small denomination checks, shop around.

In Norway, some banks charge 1 or 2 percent rather than per check. In many cases, small cash exchanges are cheaper outside of banks, at places that offer worse rates but smaller (or no) fees (such as exchange desks on international boats and the handy ForEx windows at the Copenhagen and Stockholm train stations).

American Express offices in each capital change AmExCo checks (and maybe other brands as well) for no extra fee. Even with their worse-than-banks exchange rates, those changing less than $1,000 usually save by using AmExCo. Post offices (with longer hours, nearly the same rates, and smaller fees) are a good place to change money. Don't expect to use your credit card at budget places.

Stranger in a Strange Land

We travel all the way to Europe to enjoy differences—to become temporary locals. One of the beauties of travel (especially in Scandinavia) is the opportunity to see that there are logical, civil, and even better alternatives to "truths" we always considered God-given and self-evident. While the fast and materialistic culture of America is sneaking into these countries in many ways, simplicity has yet to become subversive.

Scandinavians are into "sustainable affluence." They have experimented aggressively in the area of socialism—with mixed results. To travel here tends to pry open one's hometown blinders. Fit in, don't look for things American on the wrong side of the Atlantic, and you're sure to enjoy a full dose of Scandinavian hospitality.

Thank You

As I updated this book, revisiting my recommended hotels and private homes, I heard over and over that my readers were considerate and fun to have as guests. Thank you for traveling with sensitivity to the culture as temporary locals. It's fun to follow you in my travels.

Send Me a Postcard, Drop Me a Line

While I do what I can to keep this book accurate and up-to-date, things are always changing. If you enjoy a successful trip with the help of this book and would like to share your discoveries, please send any tips, recommendations, criticisms, or corrections to me at: Europe Through the Back Door, Box 2009, Edmonds, WA 98020. To update the book before your trip or to share tips, tap into our free computer bulletin board travel information service (206/771-1902:1200 or 2400/8/N/1). All correspondents will receive a 2-year subscription to our "Back Door Travel" quarterly newsletter (it's free anyway).

Judging from the positive feedback and happy postcards I receive from travelers using this book, it's safe to assume you're on your way to a great Scandinavian vacation—independent, inexpensive, and experienced with the finesse of a seasoned traveler. Thanks, and *happy travels!*

BACK DOOR TRAVEL PHILOSOPHY
As Taught in *Rick Steves' Europe Through the Back Door*

Travel is intensified living—maximum thrills per minute and one of the last great sources of legal adventure. Travel is freedom. It's recess, and we need it.

Experiencing the real Europe requires catching it by surprise, going casual . . . "Through the Back Door."

Affording travel is a matter of priorities. (Make do with the old car.) You can travel—simple, safe, and comfortable—anywhere in Europe for $50 a day plus transportation costs. In many ways, spending more money only builds a thicker wall between you and what you came to see. Europe is a cultural carnival, and time after time, you'll find that its best acts are free and the best seats are the cheap ones.

A tight budget forces you to travel close to the ground, meeting and communicating with the people, not relying on service with a purchased smile. Never sacrifice sleep, nutrition, safety, or cleanliness in the name of budget. Simply enjoy the local-style alternatives to expensive hotels and restaurants.

Extroverts have more fun. If your trip is low on magic moments, kick yourself and make things happen. If you don't enjoy a place, maybe you don't know enough about it. Seek the truth. Recognize tourist traps. Give a culture the benefit of your open mind. See things as different but not better or worse. Any culture has much to share.

Of course, travel, like the world, is a series of hills and valleys. Be fanatically positive and militantly optimistic. If something's not to your liking, change your liking. Travel is addicting. It can make you a happier American, as well as a citizen of the world. Our Earth is home to nearly 6 billion equally important people. It's humbling to travel and find that people don't envy Americans. They like us, but with all due respect, they wouldn't trade passports.

Globe-trotting destroys ethnocentricity. It helps you understand and appreciate different cultures. Travel changes people. It broadens perspectives and teaches new ways to measure quality of life. Many travelers toss aside their hometown blinders. Their prized souvenirs are the strands of different cultures they decide to knit into their own character. The world is a cultural yarn shop. And Back Door Travelers are weaving the ultimate tapestry. Come on, join in!

COPENHAGEN

Copenhagen (Kobenhavn) is Scandinavia's largest city. With around a million people, it's home to more than a quarter of all Danes. A busy day cruising the canals, wandering through its palace, taking a historic walk, and strolling the Stroget (Europe's greatest pedestrian shopping mall), will get you oriented and you'll feel right at home. Copenhagen is Scandinavia's cheapest and most fun-loving capital, so live it up.

Denmark

Orientation

Nearly all of your sightseeing is in Copenhagen's compact old town. By doing things on foot you'll stumble into some surprisingly cozy corners, one of the charms of Copenhagen that many miss. Study the map. The medieval walls are now roads that define the center: Vestervoldgade (literally, western wall street), Norrevoldgade, and Ostervoldgade. The fourth side is the harbor and the island of Slotsholmen where *Koben havn* (merchants' harbor) was born in 1167. The next of the city's islands is Amager, where you'll find the local "Little Amsterdam" district of Christianshavn. What was Copenhagen's moat is now a string of pleasant lakes and parks, including Tivoli Gardens. To the north is the old "new town" where the Amalienborg Palace is surrounded by streets on a grid plan and the Little Mermaid poses relentlessly, waiting for her sailor to return and the tourists to leave.

The core of the town, as far as most visitors are concerned, is the axis formed by the train station, Tivoli Gardens, the Radhus (city hall) square, and the Stroget pedestrian street. It's a great walking town, bubbling with street life and colorful pedestrian zones.

Planning Your Time

A decent first visit needs two days.

Day 1: Get set up around 9:00. If staying there, browse Christianshavn, Copenhagen's "little Amsterdam." At 10:00 explore the subterranean Christiansborg Castle ruins under today's palace. At 11:00 take the 50-minute guided tour of Denmark's royal Christiansborg Palace. At 12:00 catch the harbor tour boat for a relaxing cruise out to the mermaid. 13:30 have a buffet lunch at Riz-Raz. Visit the Use-It information center. Tour the Rosenborg Castle and crown jewels. Siesta in the park. Take the "Heart and Soul" walk described below as you shop and stroll the Stroget pedestrian mall. Evening at Tivoli Gardens (or tomorrow evening, if killing time before catching a night train out).

Day 2: Catch the 10:30 city walking tour or tour the Ny Carlsberg Glyptotek art gallery. Smorrebrod lunch. Trace Denmark's cultural roots in the National Museum. The afternoon is free with many options, including a brewery tour, Nazi Resistance museum (free tour often at 14:00), Thorvaldsen's Museum, or the Amalienborg Palace square,

With three days, side trip out to Roskilde and Fredericksborg. Remember the efficiency of sleeping in-and-out by train. If flying in, most flights from the states arrive in the morning. After that, head for Stockholm and Oslo. Kamikaze sightseers see Copenhagen as a Scandinavian bottle-neck. They sleep in-and-out heading north and in-and-out heading south with two days in, and no nights in the city. Considering the joy of Oslo and Stockholm, this isn't that crazy if you have limited time. You can check your bag at the station and take a 10-kr shower in the Interail Center.

You could set yourself up in my best rooms for your entire Scandinavian tour with a quick trip to the Telecom center in the train station.

Tourist Information

The tourist office (across from the train station on the corner of Vesterbrogade and Bernstorffsgade, next to the Tivoli entrance, tel. 33 11 13 25, daily June-mid-September 9:00-20:00; mid-September-May 9:00-16:00, Saturday 9:00-14:00, closed Sunday) is now run by a for-profit consortium called "Wonderful Copenhagen." This colors the advice and information it provides. Still, it's worth a quick stop for the top-notch freebies it provides (city map and *Copenhagen This Week*). Corporate dictates prohibit them from freely offering other brochures, but ask and you shall receive (walking tour schedules and brochures on any sights of special interest). Thinking ahead, get information and ferry schedules for your entire trip in Denmark (Frederiksborg Castle, Louisiana Museum, Kronborg Castle, Roskilde, Odense, Aero, Arhus, and Legoland).

Copenhagen This Week, a free, handy, and misnamed monthly guide to the city, is worth reading for its good maps, museum hours with telephone numbers, sightseeing tour ideas, shopping ideas, and calendar of events (free English tours and concerts). The TI's room-finding service charges you and the hotel a fee and cannot give hard opinions. Do not use it. Get on the phone and call direct (everyone speaks English).

Use It is a better information service. This "branch" of Huset, a hip, city government-sponsored, student-run cluster of cafés, theaters, and galleries, caters to Copenhagen's young, but welcomes travelers of any age. It's a friendly, driven-to-help, and energetic no-nonsense source of budget travel information, with a free room-finding service, ride-finding board, cheap transportation deals, free luggage storage, pen-pals-wanted scrapbook, free condoms, lockers, and Copenhagen's best free city maps. Their free *Playtime* publication is full of Back-Door-style travel articles on Copenhagen and the Danish culture,special budget tips, and events. They have brochures onjust about everything, including self-guided tours for bikers, walkers, and those riding scenic bus #6. They have a list of private rooms (200 kr doubles without breakfast). Open daily 9:00-19:00 mid-June-mid-September; Monday-Friday 10:00-16:00 the rest of the year. Use It is a 10-minute walk from the station, down Stroget, right on Radhustraede for 3 blocks to #13, tel. 33 15 65 18. After hours, their night board lists the cheapest rooms available in town.

The **Copenhagen Card** covers the public transportation system and admissions to nearly all the sights in greater Copenhagen, which stretches from Helsingor to Roskilde. It covers virtually all the city sights, Tivoli, and the bus in from the airport. Available at any tourist office (including the airport's) and the central station: 1 day, 140 kr; 2 days, 230 kr; 3 days, 295 kr. The sights you're likely to see are included: Christiansborg Palace (30 kr), Palace Ruins (15 kr), National Museum (30 kr), Ny Carlsberg Glyptotek (15 kr), Rosenborg Castle (35 kr), Tivoli (38 kr), Frederiksborg Castle (30 kr), and Roskilde Viking Ships (30 kr). Plus round-trip train rides to Roskilde (70 kr) and Frederiksborg Castle (70 kr). It's hard to break even, unless you're planing to side-trip on the included (and otherwise expensive) rail service. It comes with a handy book explaining the 57 included sights.

Getting Into and Around Copenhagen

Arriving by Train

Most travelers arrive in Copenhagen after an overnight train ride. The station has two long-hours money exchange desks. Den Dansk Bank (7:00-22:00 daily) is fair (charging the standard 40 kr minimum or 20 kr per check fee for travelers checks). ForEx (8:00-21:00 daily), with a worse rate but charging only 10 kr per travelers check with no minimum, is better

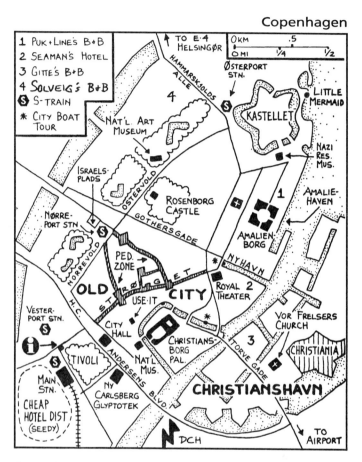

Copenhagen

1	PUK + LINE'S B+B
2	SEAMAN'S HOTEL
3	GITTE'S B+B
4	SOLVEIG'S B+B
Ⓢ	S-TRAIN
✳	CITY BOAT TOUR

for small exchanges. On $100 exchange, I saved 22 kr at ForEx. While you're in the station, reserve your overnight train seat or couchette out (at *rejsebureau*). Long rides require reservations. Between the escalators to tracks 6 and 7 are great charts of the station. These show you exactly where to catch which buses. Bus #8 (in front of the station on the station side of Bernstorffsgade) goes to Christianshavn B&Bs. Note the time the bus departs. The TI is across the street on the left.

Flights

Copenhagen's International Airport is a traveler's dream, with a tourist office, bank (standard rates), post office, telephone center, shopping mall, grocery store, bakery, and rest cabins. You can use American cash at the airport and get change back in kroner. (Airport info tel. 31 54 17 01, flight info tel. 31 54 17 01, SAS tel. 32 00, British Air tel. 31 51 30 17.)

Getting from Airport to Downtown

Taxis are fast and easy, and at about 140 kr to the town center, a good deal for foursomes. The SAS **shuttle bus** will zip you to the central train station in 20 minutes for 28 kr. **City bus** #32 gets you downtown (city hall square, TI) in 40 minutes for 15 kr (4/hr, across the street and to the right as you exit the airport). If you're going to the recommended rooms in Christianshavn, ride #9 just past Christianshavn Torv to the last stop before Knippels bridge.

If you need to kill a night at the airport, try the fetal rest cabins (SBWC-250 kr, DBWC-375 kr, rented by the 8-hour period, CC:VMA, reservations same day only, tel. 32 50 93 33, extension 2455; reception open 6:00-22:30).

Trains

Hovedbanegarden, the main train station (learn that word—you'll need to recognize it), is a temple of travel and a hive of travel-related activity. You'll find lockers (20 kr/day), a "*garderobe*" (35 kr per day per rucksack), a post office, a modern telecommunication center (above the post office, daily 8:00-22:00, Saturday and Sunday 9:00-21:00; easy, fair long-distance phone booths and rentable office services), a grocery store (daily 8:00-24:00), 24-hour thievery, bike rentals, and the Interail Center. The Interail Center, a service the station offers to mostly young travelers (but anyone with a Eurailpass, Scanrail, student BIGE or Transalpino ticket, or Interail pass is welcome) is a very pleasant lounge with 10 kr showers, free (if risky) luggage storage, city maps, snacks, information, and other young travelers (June-September 6:30-24:00). If you just need the map and "Play Time," a visit here is quicker than the TI. Train info tel. 33 14 17 01.

Public Buses and Subways

Take advantage of the fine bus (tel. 36 45) and subway system called S-tog (Eurail valid on S-tog, tel. 33 14 17 01). A joint fare system covers greater Copenhagen. You pay 10 kr as you board for an hour's travel within two zones, or buy a blue two-zone *klipkort* from the driver (70 kr for 10 1-hr "rides"). A 24-hour pass costs 65 kr. Don't worry much about "zones." Assume you'll be within the middle two zones. Board at the front, tell the driver where you're going, and he'll sell you the appropriate ticket. Drivers are patient, have change, and speak English. City maps list bus and subway routes. Locals are friendly and helpful.

HT Sightseeing Bus
This bus makes a circular route stopping at nine top Copenhagen sights (2/hr, 10:00-16:30, mid-June-August, 20 kr for 24-hour ticket). Scenic bus #6 (10 kr for an hour of stop and go) starts at the Carlsberg Brewery and stops at Tivoli, the town hall, the national museum, palace, Nyhavn, Amalienborg castle, the Kastellet, and the Little Mermaid—all described in a free, easy-to-follow Use It brochure.

Taxis
Taxis are plentiful and easy to flag down (15 kr drop charge, then 7 kr per km). For a short ride, four people can travel cheaper by taxi than by bus (e.g., 40 kr from train station to Christianshavn B&Bs.)

Bike Rental
Copenhagen is a joy on a rental bike. Use It has a great biking guide brochure and information about city bike tours (2 hrs, 50 kr including bike, grunge-approach). You can rent bikes at Central Station's Cykelcenter (open 7:00-19:00, Saturday 9:00-15:00, closed Sunday, tel. 33 14 07 17) and Dan Wheel (2 blocks from the station at 3 Colbjornsensgade, on the corner of Vesterbrogade, open 8:00-18:30, Saturday and Sunday 8:00-14:00, 40 kr/day, 60 kr/2 days, tel. 31 21 22 27).

Helpful Hints
Ferries: Book any ferries you plan to use in Scandinavia now. Any travel agent can book the boat rides you plan to take later on your trip, such as the Denmark-Norway ferry (ask for special discounts on this crossing) or the Stockholm-Helsinki-Stockholm cruise (the Silja Line office is directly

across from the station at Vesterbrogade 6D, open Monday-Friday 9:00-16:30, tel. 33 14 40 80). Drivers heading to Sweden via Helsingor should get a reservation for the ferry (tel. 33 14 88 80, and wait through the Danish recording).

Festivals: Expect extra fun and crowds in Copenhagen during its festival times—Carnival in late May, the Roskilde Rock Festival in early July, and the Copenhagen Jazz Festival for ten days starting the first Friday in July.

Telephones: Use the telephone liberally. Phone booths are everywhere, calls are 1 kr, everyone speaks English, and *This Week* and this book list phone numbers for everything you'll be doing. All telephone calls in Denmark, even local ones, must include eight digits. There are no area codes. Calls anywhere in Denmark are cheap. Calls to Norway and Sweden cost 6 kr per minute from a booth (half that from a home). Since so many booths don't work, get a phone card (starting at 20 kr from newsstands).

Traveler's Checks: The American Express Company (Stroget at Amagertorv 18, Monday-Friday 9:00-17:00, Saturday 9:00-12:00, tel. 33 12 23 01) does not charge the 40 kr fees on their checks (or sometimes on any checks).

Sights—Copenhagen

Orientation Walk: "Copenhagen's Heart and Soul"— Start from Radhuspladsen (City Hall Square), the bustling heart of Copenhagen, dominated by the City Hall spire. This used to be the fortified west end of town. The king cleverly quelled a French revolutionary-type thirst for democracy by giving his people Europe's first great public amusement park. Tivoli was built just outside the city walls in 1843. When the train lines came, the station was placed just beyond Tivoli. The golden girls high up on the building opposite the square tell the weather: on a bike or with an umbrella.

Old Hans Christian Andersen sits to the right of the city hall almost begging to be in another photo (as he did in real life). On a pedestal left of the City Hall, note the Lur-Blowers sculpture. The *lur* is a horn that was used 3,500 years ago. The ancient originals (which still play) are displayed in the National Museum and depicted on most tiny butter tubs.

From the less ancient Burger King stretches Copenhagen's main—and Europe's first—pedestrian street, Stroget.

Stroget (stroy-et) is actually a series of colorful streets and lively squares that bunny-hop through the old town, connecting the City Hall Square with Kongens Nytorv (The King's New Square, a 15-minute walk away)

The most historic bits and pieces of old Copenhagen are just off this commercial can-can. At the end of the first segment, Frederiksberggade, you'll hit Gammel Torv and Nytorv (old and new square). This was the old town center. The Oriental-looking kiosk was one of the city's first community telephone centers before phones were privately owned. The very old fountain was so offensive to people from the Victorian age that the pedestal was added, raising it—hopefully—out of view. The brick church at the start of Amager Torv is the oldest building you'll see here.

The final stretch of Stroget leads past the American Express office and major department stores, to the king's new square (Kongens Nytorv) where you'll find the Royal Theater and Nyhavn, a recently gentrified sailors' quarter. This formerly sleazy harbor is an interesting mix of tattoo parlors, taverns, and trendy (mostly expensive) cafés lining a canal filled with glamorous old sailboats of all sizes. Any historic sloop is welcome to moor here in Copenhagen's ever-changing boat museum. Hans Christian Andersen lived here and wrote his first stories here.

Continuing north, along the harborside, you'll pass a huge ship that sails to Oslo every evening. Follow the water to the modern fountain of Amaliehaven Park. The nearby Amalienborg Palace and Square is a good example of orderly baroque planning. Queen Margrethe II and her family live in the palace to your immediate left as you enter the square from the harbor side. Her son and heir to the throne, Frederik, recently moved into the palace directly opposite his mother's. While the guards change with royal fanfare at noon only when the queen is in residence, they shower every morning.

Leave the square on Amaliegade, heading north to Kastellet (Citadel) Park and a small museum about Denmark's World War II resistance efforts. A short stroll, past the Gefion fountain (showing the mythological story of the carving of Denmark out of Sweden) and a church made of flint and along the water, brings you to the overrated and over-photographed symbol of Copenhagen—the Little Mermaid.

Central Copenhagen

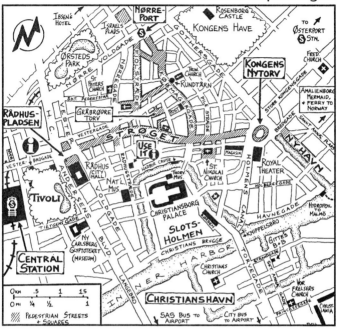

You can get back downtown on foot, by taxi, or on bus #1, #6 or #9 from Store Kongensgade on the other side of Kastellet Park (a special bus may run from the Mermaid in summer).

▲**Copenhagen's Town Hall (Radhus)**—This city landmark, between the station/Tivoli/TI and Stroget pedestrian mall, offers private tours and trips up its 350-foot-high tower. The city hall is open to the public (free, Monday-Friday, 10:00-15:00). Tours are given in English and get you into otherwise-closed rooms (20 kr, 45 minutes, daily 15:00, Saturday 10:00). Tourists are allowed to romp up the tower's 300 steps for the best aerial view of Copenhagen (10 kr, Monday-Friday 10:00, 12:00, and 14:00; Saturday 12:00; off-season 12:00, tel. 33 66 25 82).

▲**Christiansborg Palace**—This modern *slot*, or palace, built on the ruins of the original 12th-century palace, houses the parliament, supreme court, prime minister's headquarters, and royal reception rooms. Guided 40-minute English tours

of the Queen's reception rooms (27 kr, May-September,
Tuesday-Sunday at 11:00, 13:00, 15:00; off-season Tuesday,
Thursday, and Sunday 11:00 and 15:00; tel. 33 92 64 92) let
you slip-slide on protect-the-floor slippers through 22 rooms
and gain a good feel for Danish history, royalty, and politics
in this 100-year-old, still-functioning palace. For a run down
on contemporary government, you can also tour the parliament building. From the equestrian statue in front, go
through the wooden door, past the entrance to the
Christianborg Castle ruins, into the courtyard, and up
the stairs on the right.

▲**Christiansborg Castle Ruins**—An exhibit in the scant
remains of the first castle built by Bishop Absalon—the 12th-
century founder of Copenhagen—lies under the palace. (15
kr, daily 9:30-15:30, closed off-season Monday and Saturday,
good 1 kr guide). Early birds note that this sight opens 30
minutes before other nearby sights.

▲▲▲**National Museum**—Focus on the excellent and curi-
ously enjoyable Danish collection, which traces this civiliza-
tion from its ancient beginnings, laid out on the ground floor
chronologically starting with the "prehistory" section. Very
good English explanations make highlights such as the passage graves, mummified Viking bodies with their armor and
weapons, the 2,000-year-old Gunderstrup Caldron, original
ancient *lur* horns, Viking gear, mead drinking horns,
medieval church art, and domestic furniture particularly
interesting. (30 kr, enter from Ny Vestergade, open 10:00-
17:00, closed Monday, tel. 33 13 44 11, extension 460; occasional free English tours in the summer, call first.)

▲**Ny Carlsberg Glyptotek**—Scandinavia's top art gallery,
with an especially intoxicating Egyptian, Greek, and
Etruscan collection, the best of Danish Golden Age (early
19th-century) painting, and a heady, if small, exhibit of 19th-
century French paintings (Gericault, Delacroix, Manet,
impressionists, Gauguin before and after Tahiti) is an
impressive example of what beer money can do. Linger
under the palm leaves and glass dome of the very soothing
conservatory. One of the original Rodin *Thinker*s can be seen
for free (wondering how to scale the Tivoli fence?) in the
museum's backyard. (15 kr, free on Wednesday and Sunday,
behind Tivoli, open Tuesday-Sunday 10:00-16:00, off-season

12:00-15:00; occasional free English tours, tel. 33 41 81 41.) This is particularly important if you've not seen the great galleries of central Europe.

▲▲▲**Tivoli Gardens**—The world's most famous amusement park is 150 years old. It is 20 acres, 110,000 lanterns, and countless ice cream cones of fun. You pay one 38 kr admission price and find yourself lost in a Hans Christian Andersen wonderland of rides, restaurants, games, marching bands, roulette wheels, and funny mirrors. Tivoli is wonderfully Danish. It doesn't try to be Disney. (Open 10:00-24:00, late April-mid-September, closed off-season, 27 kr entry until 13:00, all children's amusements in full swing 11:30-22:00; all amusements open 13:30; events on the half hour 18:30-23:00; concert in the concert hall at 19:30 for 40 kr-140 kr, tel. 33 15 10 01.) Go in with a full stomach or a discreet picnic (the food inside is costly). If you must eat inside, there are cheap Polser stands. **Faergekroen** is a good lakeside place for a beer or some typical Danish food. The Yugoslavian restaurant, **Hercegovina**, is a decent value (110 kr buffet). For a reasonable cake and coffee try the **Viften** café.

Pick up a map and schedule as you enter and locate a billboard schedule of events (British flag for English). Free concerts, mime, ballet, acrobats, puppets, and other shows pop up all over the park, and a well-organized visitor can enjoy an exciting evening of entertainment without spending a single krone (though occasionally the schedule is a bit sparse). If the Tivoli Symphony is playing, it's worth paying for. Rides are reasonable, but the all-day pass for 160 kr is probably best for those who may have been whirling dervishes in a previous life. On Wednesday, Friday, and Saturday the place closes down (at 23:45) with a fireworks show. If you're taking an overnight train out of Copenhagen, Tivoli (just across from the station) is the place to spend your last Copenhagen hours.

▲▲**Rosenborg Castle**—This impressively furnished Renaissance-style castle houses the Danish crown jewels and 500 years of royal knickknacks. It's musty with history. Pick up and follow the 1 kr guide page. The castle is surrounded by the royal gardens, a rare plant collection, and on sunny days, a minefield of sunbathing Danish beauties. (35 kr, daily June-August 10:00-16:00; May, September, and October

11:00-15:00; off-season Tuesday, Friday, and Sunday 11:00-
14:00; there's no electricity inside so visit at a bright time,
tel. 33 15 32 86, S-train: Norreport.) There is a daily changing of the guard mini-parade from Rosenborg Castle (at
11:30) to Amalienborg Castle (at 12:00).

▲**Denmark's Fight for Freedom Museum
(Frihedsmuseet)**—The fascinating story of a heroic Nazi
resistance struggle is well explained in English. (free, between
the Queen's Palace and the Mermaid, daily May to mid-
September 10:00-16:00, closed Mondays; off-season 11:00-
15:00, tel. 33 13 77 14, bus #1, #6, or #9.)

▲▲▲**Stroget**—Copenhagen's 25-year-old experimental,
tremendously successful, and most copied pedestrian shopping mall is a string of serendipitous streets and lovely
squares from the city hall to Nyhavn. Spend some time
browsing, people-watching, and exploring both here and
along adjacent pedestrian-only streets. The commercial focus
of an historic street like Stroget drives up the land value,
which generally tears down the old buildings. While Stroget
has become quite hamburgerized, charm lurks in many adjacent areas, such as nearby Grabrodtorv (Grey Brothers'
Square). Straedet ("the street") is Copenhagen's newly
pedestrianized street running parallel to Stroget on the water
side. (For more on Stroget, see the Orientation Walk above.)
Stroget is not an actual street but the popular name for a
series of individually named streets. Many of the best night
spots are just off Stroget. The best department stores
(Illum's and Magazin, see below) are on Stroget.

▲**Copenhagen Walking Tour**—Once upon a time,
American Richard Karpen visited Copenhagen and fell in
love with the city (and one of its women). He gives daily 2-
hour walking tours of his adopted home town covering its
people, history, and the contemporary scene. His entertaining one-language walks (there are three covering different
parts of the city center) leave daily (May-September) from in
front of the TI (30 kr, pick up schedule at the TI or Use It,
tel. 32 97 14 40). Richard and the local historian Helge
Jacobsen (tel. 31 51 25 90) give reasonably priced private
walks and tours.

▲▲**Harbor Cruise and Canal Tours**—Two companies
offer basically the same live, four-language, 60-minute tours

through the city canals (2/hr, 10:00-17:00, later in July, May to mid-September). They cruise around the palace and Christianshavn area, into the wide open harbor, and out to the Mermaid. Both leave from near Christiansborg Palace. It's a pleasant way to see the Mermaid and take a load off those weary sightseeing feet. Dress warm; boats are open-top.

The low-overhead 15 kr Netto-Badene Tour boats (tel. 31 54 41 02) leave from Holmens Kirke across from the Borsen (stock exchange) just over Knippels bridge. The competition, a 36 kr harbor tour with a cheaper unguided ride, leaves from Gammel Strand near Christiansborg Palace and National Museum, tel. 33 13 31 05. Don't be confused. There's no reason to pay double for their tour. Boats can also be boarded at Nyhavn.

▲**Vor Frelsers (Our Savior's) Church**—The church's bright baroque interior is worth a look (free, daily June-August 9:00-16:30, Sunday 13:00-16:30; closes an hour early in spring and fall; off-season 10:00-13:30, tel. 31 57 27 98, bus #8). The unique spiral spire that you'll admire from afar can be climbed for a great city view and a good aerial view of the Christiania commune below. It's 311 feet high, claims to have 400 steps, costs 10 kr, and is closed through 1996 for restoration.

Christiania—This is a unique on-again, off-again social experiment, a counterculture utopia attempt that is, to many, disillusioning. An ultra-human mishmash of 1,000 idealists, anarchists, hippies, dope fiends, non-materialists, and people who dream only of being a Danish bicycle seat has established squatters' rights in a former military barracks (follow the beer bottles and guitars down Prinsessegade behind Vor Frelsers' spiral church spire in Christianshavn). This communal cornucopia of dogs, dirt, drugs, and dazed people—or haven of peace, freedom, and no taxes, depending on your perspective—is a political hot potato. No one in the establishment wants it—or has the nerve to mash it. While hard drugs are out, hash and pot are sold openly (with senior discounts) and smoked happily.

Past the souvenir and hash-vendor entry you'll find a fascinating ramshackle world of moats and ramparts, alternative housing, unappetizing falafel stands, crispy hash browns, a good restaurant (Spiseloppen), handicraft shops, and filth. If you visit, make a point to get off the main "pusher street."

Christiania's most motley inhabitants are low-life vagabonds from other countries who hang out here in the summer. Now that Christiania is no longer a teenager, it's making an effort to connect better with the rest of society. The community is paying its utilities and even offering daily walking tours. Its free English/Dansk visitor's magazine, *Nitten* (available at Use It), is good reading, offering a serious explanation about how this unique community works/survives. It suggests several do-it-yourself walking tours.

Carlsberg Brewery Tour—Denmark's two beloved sources of legal intoxicants, Carlsberg and Tuborg, offer free 1-hour brewery tours followed by 30-minute "tasting sessions." Carlsberg tour: Monday-Friday 11:00 and 14:00 (bus #6 to 140 Ny Carlsberg Vej, tel. 33 27 13 14, ext. 1312). Tuborg tour: Monday-Friday 10:00, 12:30, and 14:30 (bus #6 to Strandvejen 54, Hellerup, tel. 33 27 22 12).

Museum of Erotica—This museum offers a chance to visit a porno shop and call it a museum. It took some digging, but they have documented a history of sex from Pompeii to present day. Visitors get a peep into the world of 19th-century Copenhagen prostitutes, a chance to read up on the sex lives of Martin Luther, Queen Elizabeth, Charlie Chaplin, Casanova (and others), and the arguably artistic experience of watching the "electric tabernakel," (12 busy but silent screens of porn to the accompaniment of classical music). Not worth the 45 kr entry fee but better than the Amsterdam equivalents, just past Tivoli at Vesterbrogade 31, daily 10:00-23:00 May-September; 12:00-18:00 the rest of the year, tel. 33 12 03 11). For the real thing—and free—wander Copenhagen's dreary little red-light district along Istedgade behind the train station.

Hovedbanegarden—The great Copenhagen train station is a fascinating mesh of Scandimanity and transportation efficiency. Even if you're not a train traveler, check it out (fuller description in Orientation, above).

Other Sights to Consider

Torvaldsens Museum (free, next to Christiansborg Palace, 10:00-17:00, closed Monday) features the early 18th-century work of Denmark's greatest sculptor. The noontime **changing of the guard** at the Amalienborg Palace is boring: all they change is places. **Nyhavn**, with its fine old ships, tattoo shops (pop into Tattoo Ole at #17—fun photos, very traditional), and jazz clubs, is a wonderful place to hang out. Copenhagen's **Open Air Folk Museum** is a park filled with traditional Danish architecture and folk culture (30 kr, S-train to Sorgenfri, open April-October 10:00-17:00, closed Monday; shorter hours off-season, tel. 42 85 02 92). Organized **bus tours** of the city leave from the Town Hall Square (1½-3 hrs, 110 kr-160 kr). The Danes gather at Copenhagen's other great amusement park, **Bakken** (free, daily April-August 14:00-24:00, 30-minutes by S-train to Klampenborg, tel. 31 63 73 00).

If you don't have time to get to the idyllic island of Aero (see chapter on Central Denmark), consider a trip to the tiny fishing village of **Dragor** (30 minutes on bus #30 or #33 from Copenhagen's City Hall Square).

Nightlife

For the latest on Copenhagen's hopping jazz scene, pick up the *Copenhagen Jazz Guide* at the TI or the more "alternative" *Playtime* magazine at Use It.

Shopping

Copenhagen's colorful **flea market** (summer Saturdays 8:00-14:00 at Israels Plads) is small but feisty and surprisingly cheap. An antique market enlivens Nybrogade (near the palace) every Friday and Saturday. Other flea markets are listed in *Copenhagen This Week*. The city's top department stores (Illum at 52 Ostergade, tel. 33 14 40 02, and Magasin at 13 Kongens Nytorv, tel. 33 11 44 33) offer a good, if expensive, look at today's Denmark. Both are on Stroget and have fine cafeterias on their top floors.

Danes shop cheaper at Daell's Varehus (corner of Krystalgade and Fiolstraede). At UFF on Kultorvet you can buy newly new clothes for peanuts and support charity. Just across Vesterbrogade from Tivoli, Scala is a new glitzy mishmash of 45 shops, lots of eateries, and entertainment. Survey Scala from its bubble elevator. Shops are open Monday-Friday 9:30/10:00-18:00/19:00; Saturday 9:00-14:00.

The department stores and the Politiken Bookstore on the Radhus Square have a good selection of maps and

English travel guides. If you buy over 600 kr ($100) worth of stuff, you can get the 25 percent VAT (MOMS in Danish) tax back (if you buy from a shop displaying the Danish Tax-Free Shopping emblem). If you have your purchase mailed, the tax can be deducted from your bill. Call 32 52 55 66, see the shopping-oriented *Copenhagen This Week*, or ask a merchant for specifics.

Sleeping in Copenhagen
(7 kr = about $1)
I've listed the best budget hotels in the center (with doubles for 400 kr-600 kr with breakfast), rooms in private homes an easy bus ride or 15-minute walk from the station (around 330 kr per double with breakfast), and the dormitory options (100 kr per person with breakfast). Unless noted, breakfast is included in the price.

Sleep code: **S**=Single, **D**=Double/Twin, **T**=Triple, **Q**=Quad, **B**=Bath/Shower, **WC**=Toilet, **CC**=Credit Card (**V**isa, **M**astercard, **A**mex).

Hotel Sankt Jorgen has big, friendly-feeling rooms with plain old wood furnishings. Brigitte and Susan offer a warm welcome and a great value (S-300 kr-350 kr, D-400 kr-450 kr, 3rd person 100 kr-125 kr extra, prices flex with the demand; breakfast served in your room, elevator, a 12-minute walk from the station or catch bus #13 to the first stop after the lake; Julius Thomsensgade 22, DK-1632 Copenhagen V, tel. 35 37 15 11, fax 35 37 11 97).

Ibsen's Hotel is a rare simple bath-down-the-hall, cheery, and central budget hotel, run by three women (there's really only two) who treat you like you're paying top dollar. (S-420 kr, D-600 kr, 3rd person-150 kr, CC: VMA, no elevator, lots of stairs; Vendersgade 23, DK 1363, tel. 33 13 19 13, fax 33 13 19 16, bus #16 or S-train: Norreport.)

Hotel KFUM Soldaterhjem, originally for soldiers, is on the fifth floor with no elevators (S-195 kr, D-310 kr without breakfast; Gothersgade 115, Copenhagen K, tel. 33 15 40 44). The reception is on the first floor up (open 8:30-23:00, weekends 15:00-23:00) next to a budget cafeteria.

Cab-Inn Copenhagen (S-395 kr, D-480 kr, T-565 kr, Q-650 kr, Danasvej 32-34, 1910 Frederiksberg C, tel.

31 21 04 00, fax 31 21 74 09, 5 minutes on bus #29 to center) is a radical innovation: 86 identical tiny but luxurious cruise ship-type staterooms, all bright and shiny with TV, video player, coffee pot, shower, and toilet. Each room has a single bed that expands into a comfortable double with 1 or 2 fold-down bunks on the walls. Breakfast, 35 kr; easy parking, 30 kr. The staff will hardly give you the time of day, but it's hard to argue with this efficiency. **Cab-Inn Scandinavia** is its twin, 400 meters away (tel. 35 36 11 11).

Hotel 9 Sma Hjem (DBWC-450 kr, CC:VMA, Classensgade 40, DK-2100 Copenhagen O, tel. 35 26 16 47, fax 35 43 17 84, 12 minutes on bus #40 from the station) is also good.

The Excelsior Hotel (DBWC-650 kr-865 kr in July and August, 4 Colbjornsensgade, DK-1652, tel. 31 24 50 85, fax 31 24 50 87) is a big, mod, tour group hotel a block behind the station. Some people like it.

Sleeping in Rooms in Private Homes

Here are a few leads for Copenhagen's best accommodation values. While each TI has its own list of B&Bs, by booking direct, you'll save yourself and your host the tourist office fee. Always call ahead. Each family speaks English.

Sleeping in Rooms in Private Homes in Christianshavn

This area is a never-a-dull-moment hodgepodge of the chic, artistic, hippie, and hobo, with beer-drinking Greenlanders littering streets in the shadow of fancy government ministries. It's handy with lots of shops, cafés, and canals, a 10-minute walk to the center, and good bus connections to the airport and downtown.

Annette and Rudy Hollender enjoy sharing their 300-year-old home with my readers. Even with sinkless rooms and three rooms sharing one toilet/shower, it's a comfortable and cheery place to call home (S-210 kr, D-270 kr, T-400 kr, breakfast-40 kr, Wildersgade 19, 1408 Copenhagen K, tel. 31 95 96 22, fax 31 57 24 86, after June 1995 tel. 32 95 96 22, fax 32 57 24 86). Take bus #9 from the airport, bus #8 from the station, or bus #2 from the City Hall. From downtown, push the button immediately after crossing Knippels Bridge, and turn left off Torvegade down Wildersgade. If Annette's place is full, she runs a network of about 20 rooms, all at the same price in this charming locale. If you have any personality quirks, she loves to play match-maker.

Morten Frederiksen, a laid-back, ponytailed sort of guy, runs a mod-funky-pleasant loft. It's a clean, comfy, good look at today's hip Danish lifestyle and has a great location right on Christianshavn's main drag (D-250 kr, 2 minutes from Annette's, Torvegade 36, tel. 31 95 32 73, after June 1995 tel. 32 95 32 73).

Solveig Diderichsen rents three rooms (D-270 kr, 3rd person-100 kr) from her comfortable home. She serves no breakfast, but offers kitchen facilities and a good bakery around the corner. Her high-ceilinged, ground-floor apartment is in a quiet embassy neighborhood behind the Oster Anlaeg park (three stops on the subway from the central station, to Osterport, then a 3-minute walk, or bus #6 or #1 from Vesterbrogade near the station, or bus #9 direct from the airport, Upsalagade 26, DK-2100, tel. 35 43 22 70 or 31 38 39 58).

Annette Haugballe rents four modern, comfortable rooms in the quiet, green, and residential Frederiksberg area (S-160 kr, D-250 kr, easy parking, Hoffmeyersvej 33, 2000 Frederiksberg, Copenhagen, tel. 31 74 87 87, on bus line #1 from station or city hall square, and near Peter Bangsvej S subway station). She also has friends who rent rooms.

Sleeping near the Amalienborg Palace

This is a stately embassy neighborhood—no stress but a bit bland. It's very safe, and you can look out your window to see the queen's place (and the guards changing), which is a 10-minute walk north of Nyhavn and Stroget. **Puk De La Cour** (D-250 kr with no breakfast but tea, coffee and a kitchen, family room available, Amaliegade 34, fourth floor, tel. 33 12 04 68) rents two rooms in her mod, bright, and easygoing house. Puk (pook)'s friend, **Line Voutsinos** (Amaliegade 34, 3rd floor, tel. 33 14 71 42), offers a similar deal.

Sleeping in Flats for Hire

Many Copenhagen residents head for their country bungalows in the summer and hire an agency to rent out their homes for a minimum of three nights. These places are mostly in the center of town, completely furnished with a kitchen and the lived-in works (TV, stereo, washer and dryer, and so on) and are a particularly good deal for families or small groups who would trade away the B&B friendliness for the privacy of this less personal alternative. **H.A.Y.4U** (near Stroget at Kronprinsensgade 10, 114 Copenhagen K, tel. 33 33 08 05, fax 33 32 08 04) takes drop-ins, but recommends that you reserve a month in advance. Rates vary from 300 kr a day for 1-bedroom places to 500 kr per day for four-person places.

Sleeping in Youth Hostels

Copenhagen energetically accommodates the young vagabond on a shoestring. The Use It office is your best source of information. Each of these places charges about 100 kr per person for bed and breakfast. Some don't allow sleeping bags, and if you don't have your own hostel bedsheet, you'll normally have to rent one for around 25 kr. IYHF hostels require a membership card, but will normally sell you a "guest pass" for 22 kr.

The modern **Copenhagen Hostel** (IYHF) is huge, with fifty 170-kr doubles and 85 5-bed dorms, no curfew, excellent facilities, cheap meals, and a self-serve laundry. Unfortunately, it's on the edge of town, bus #16 from the station to Mozartplads, then #37 or #38 (200 Vejlands Alle/Sjaellandsbroen 55, 2300 Copenhagen S, tel. 32 52 29 08).

The grungy **City Public Hostel** with 200 beds in one big room and open to all from mid-May to August (8 Absalonsgade, tel. 31 31 20 70) has only one advantage: it's a short walk from the station.

KFUK/KFUM (Danish YMCA/YWCA) has a great location in the pedestrian center with 4- to 6-bed rooms partitioned out of a big hall (July to mid-August only, closed 12:00-14:30, and at 24:00; Kannikestraede 19, behind Grabrodretorv just off Stroget, tel. 33 11 30 31,). There's a similar Y at Valdemarsgade 15 (tel. 31 31 15 74).

The Sleep-In is popular with the desperate or adventurous (July-August, 4-bed cubicles in a huge 452-bed coed room, no curfew, pretty wild, lockers, always has room; Per Henrik Lings Alle 6, tel. 35 26 50 59, S-train A, B, or C to Nordhavn near the Mermaid). Sleeping bag required. No curfew. Free rubbers. In the summer, **Jorgensens Hotel** rents beds to backpackers in small dorms (near Norreport, Romersgade 11, tel. 33 13 81 86, fax 33 15 51 05.)

Eating in Copenhagen

Copenhagen's many good restaurants are well listed by category in *Copenhagen This Week*. Since restaurant prices include 25 percent tax plus a 15 percent tip, your budget may require alternatives. These survival ideas for the hungry budget traveler in Copenhagen will save lots of money.

Picnics

Irma (in arcade next to Tivoli) and **Brugsen** are the two largest supermarket chains. **Netto** and **Aldi** are cut-rate outfits with the cheapest prices. The little grocery store in the central station (daily 8:00-24:00) is picnic-friendly.

Viktualiehandler (small delis) and bakeries, found on nearly every corner, sell fresh bread, tasty pastries (a *wienerbrod* is what we call a "Danish"), juice, milk, cheese, and yogurt (tall liter boxes, drinkable). Liver paste (*postej*) is cheap and a little better than it sounds.

Smorrebrod

Denmark's famous open-face sandwiches cost a fortune in restaurants, but the many smorrebrod shops sell them for 8 kr-26 kr. Drop into one of these often no-name, family-run budget savers, and get several elegant OFSs to go. The tradition calls for three sandwich courses: herring first, then meat, then cheese. It makes for a classy—and cheap—picnic. Downtown you'll find these handy local alternatives to Yankee fast food chains: **Centrum** (6 C. Vesterbrogade, 24 hours a day, across from station and Tivoli), **City Smorrebrod** (12 Gronnegade, open 8:00-14:00, closed Saturday and Sunday, near Kongens Nytorv), **Domhusets Smorrebrod** (18 Kattesundet, Monday-Friday 7:00-14:30), **Sorgenfri** (just off the Stroget, 8 Brolaeggerstraede, Monday-Friday 11:00-14:00), one in a basement 30 meters from Riz Raz, and one at the corner of Magstraede and Radhusstraede

(Monday-Friday, 7:00-14:30, next to Huset/Use It). There is one in Nyhavn, on the corner of Holbergsgade and Peder Skram Gade.

The Polse

The famous Danish hot dog, sold in *polsevogn* (sausage wagons) throughout the city, is one of the few typically Danish institutions to resist the onslaught of our global fast-food culture. They are fast, cheap, tasty, easy to order ("hot dog" is a Danish word for weenie, study the photo menu for variations), and almost worthless nutritionally. Still the local "dead man's finger" is the dog kids love to bite.

By hanging around a *polsevognen* you can study this institution. It's a form of social care: only difficult-to-employ people, such as the handicapped, are licensed to run these wienermobiles. As they gain seniority they are promoted to more central locations. Danes gather here for munchies and *polsesnak* (sausage talk), the local slang for empty chatter.

Inexpensive Restaurants

Riz-Raz (around the corner from Use It at 20 Kompag-nistraede) serves a healthy all-you-can eat Mediterranean buffet, 40 kr lunch (daily 11:00-17:00), and an even bigger 60 kr dinner buffet (until 23:00), which has got to be the best deal in town. And they're happy to serve free water with your meal. Department stores (especially the top floor of **Illums**, an elegant circus of reasonable food under a glass dome, **Magasin**, or **Daell's Varehus** at Norregade 12) serve cheery, reasonable meals.

Fast food joints are everywhere. Look for all-you-can-eat pizza and salad bars. **Alexander's Pizza Bar** serves all the pizza and salad you can stand for 40 kr, but they charge 8 kr for a glass of tap water (just off Stroget, between the Frue Church and the Round Tower at Lille Kannikestr 5, daily 12:00-22:30, avoid the late crowds, tel. 33 12 55 36). **Det Lille Apotek** (across the street from Alexander's) is a reasonable, candle-lit place popular with local students. Nearby on Larsbjornsstrade (a hip and color-ful, trendy street), **Istanbul Pizza** sells delicious 10 kr/slice pizza.

Koldt Bord

For a fun, affordable way to explore your way through a world of traditional Danish food, try a Danish smorgasbord (an all-you-can-eat buffet). The handiest is the famous Koldt Bord at the central station's **Bistro Restaurant** (130 kr dinner, served daily 11:30-21:30, tel. 33 14 12 32). As their ad brags, "There are more specialties than you can overcome." Use a new plate with each course. The food is laid out chronologically. Start opposite the desserts and work your way through pickled herring, cold cuts, soup, hot meat and vegetables, cheese, and dessert. They also offer a special daily dinner plate for 50 kr-60 kr and happily serve free tap water.

Good Eating in Christianshavn

Cafe Wilder (corner of Wildersgade and Skt Annae Gade, a block off Torvegade) serves creative and hearty dinner salads by candle light to a trendy local clientele. To avoid having to choose just one of their interesting salads, try their three salads plate (55 kr with bread). They also feature a budget dinner plate for around 60 kr and are happy to serve free water. Across the street, the **Luna Cafe** is also good.

Locals like the **La Novo** Italian restaurant (Torvegade 49), where the 50 kr lasagna is a meal in itself. The **Cibi E Vini** take-out deli (Torvegade 28, near the bridge, daily 10:00-18:00, Saturday 10:00-14:00) serves take-out sandwiches and pastas. Right on the community square, you'll find a huge grocery store, fruit stands under the Greenlanders monument, and a great bakery (at the bus stop, Torvegade 45). The **Ravelin Restaurant** (Torvegade 79) serves good traditional Danish-style food at reasonable prices to happy local crowds on a lovely lakeside terrace (only on sunny days).

Eating Downtown

Parnas (live piano sing-song almost every night at 21:30, Lille Kongensgade 4, tel. 33 12 12 24) and **Skindbuksen** (Lille Kongensgade 4, tel. 33 12 90 37) are both cozy, atmospheric, dark, reasonable, popular with locals, and just off Stroget. **Vin and Olgod** (Skindergade 45, 19:00-02:00, closed Sunday and Monday, tel. 33 13 26 25) is the place to go for old-time sing, dance, eat, and drink rowdiness. For an idyllic wooded break from the city, in the city, find **Roberta's Cafe** for hearty pita salads (in the northeast corner of Orsteds Park).

Transportation Connections
Copenhagen to: Hillerod/Frederiksborg (40/day, 30 min), **Louisiana** (Helsinger train to Humlebaek, 40/day, 30 min), **Roskilde** (16/day, 30 min), **Odense** (16/day, 3 hrs), **Helsingor** (ferry to Sweden, 40/day, 30 min), **Stockholm** (8/day, 8 hrs), **Oslo** (4/day, 10 hrs), **Vaxjo** (via Alvesta, 6/day, 5 hrs), **Kalmar** (6/day, via Alvesta and Vaxjo, 7 hrs), **Berlin** (via Gedser, 2/day, 9 hrs), **Amsterdam** (2/day, 11 hrs), **Frankfurt/Rhine** (4/day, 10 hrs).

Cheaper **bus trips** are listed at Use It. All Norway and Sweden trains go right onto the Helsingor-Helsingborg ferry. The crossing and reservation are included on any train ticket. There are convenient overnight trains from Copenhagen directly to Stockholm, Oslo, Berlin, Amsterdam, and Frankfurt.

A quickie cruise from Copenhagen to Oslo: A luxurious cruise ship leaves daily from Copenhagen (departs 17:00, returns 9:15 two days later; 16 hours sailing each way and 7 hours in Norway's capital). Special packages give you a bed in a double cabin, a fine dinner, and two smorgasbord breakfasts for around $200 in summer. Cheaper on Sunday-Thursday departures and after August 22. Call DFDS Scandinavian Seaways (tel. 33 15 76 96). It's easy to make a reservation in the U.S.A. (tel. 800/5DF-DS56).

Near Copenhagen: Roskilde, Hillerod, Frederiksborg Castle, Louisiana, Helsingor, Kronborg Castle
Copenhagen's the star but there are several worthwhile sights nearby, and the public transportation system makes side-tripping a joy. Visit Roskilde's great Viking ships and royal cathedral. Tour Frederiksborg, Denmark's most spectacular castle. And ponder the cutting edge at Louisiana, a superb art museum with a coastal setting as striking as its art. At Helsingor, do the dungeons of Kronborg Castle before heading on to Sweden.

Greater Copenhagen

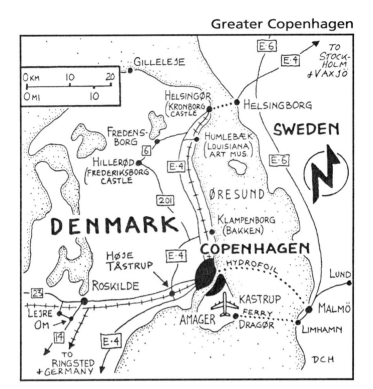

Planning Your Time

Roskilde's Viking ships and the Frederiksborg Palace are the area's essential sights. Each (an easy 30-minute commute from Copenhagen followed by a 15-minute walk) can be done in half a day. You'll find fewer tour bus crowds in the afternoon. While you're in Roskilde, pay your respects to the tombs of the Danish royalty. By car, you'll do them on your way in or out of Copenhagen. By train, do side trips when you can sleep through them to and from Copenhagen to heavyweight sights 8 or 10 hours away.

Roskilde

Denmark's roots, both Viking and royal, are on display in Roskilde, a pleasant town 20 miles west of Copenhagen. Five hundred years ago, Roskilde was Denmark's leading city.

Today, the town that introduced Christianity to Denmark in A.D.980 is most famous for hosting northern Europe's biggest annual rock/jazz/folk festival (four days in early July). Wednesday and Saturday are flea/flower/produce market days. Its TI next to the cathedral (tel. 42 35 27 00) is helpful. Roskilde is an easy side trip from Copenhagen by train (30 minutes, several per hour).

Sights—Roskilde

▲▲**Roskilde Cathedral**—Roskilde's imposing 12th-century, twin-spired cathedral houses the tombs of 38 Danish kings and queens. It's a stately, modern-looking old church with great marble work, paintings (notice the impressive 3-D painting with Christian IV looking like a pirate, in the room behind the small pipe organ), wood carvings in and around the altar, and the silly little glockenspiel (that plays high above the entrance at the top of every hour). The 20 kr guidebook is very good. (5 kr admission, open April-September 9:00-16:45; off-season 10:00-15:00, Sunday from 12:30.) It's a pleasant walk through a park down to the harbor and Viking ships.

▲▲▲**Viking Ship Museum** (Vikingeskibshallen)—Roskilde's award-winning museum displays five different Viking ships—one is like the boat Leif Ericsson sailed to America 1,000 years ago, another is like those depicted in the Bayeux Tapestry. The descriptions are excellent—and in English. It's the kind of museum where you want to read everything. As you enter, buy the 2 kr guide booklet and request the 15-minute English movie introduction. These ships were deliberately sunk 1,000 years ago to block a nearby harbor and were only recently excavated, preserved, and pieced together. The ships aren't as intact as those in Oslo, butthe museum does a better job explaining shipbuilding. The museum cafeteria serves the original Vikingburger (28 kr)—great after a hard day of pillage, plunder, or sightseeing. (30 kr entry, open April-October 9:00-17:00, November-March 10:00-16:00, tel. 42 35 65 55.)

Hillerod

The traffic-free center of this Danishly cute town (just outside the gates of the mighty Frederiksborg Castle, past the

Tourist Information office) is worth a wander (TI tel. 42 26
28 52, can book rooms in private homes for 125 kr per person and 30 kr per breakfast).

Sights—Hillerod

▲▲Frederiksborg Castle—This grandest castle in Scandinavia is often called the Danish Versailles. Frederiksborg (built 1602-1620) is the castle of Christian IV, Denmark's great builder king. You can almost hear the cackle
of royal hoofbeats as you walk over the moat through the
stately cobbled courtyard, past the Dutch Renaissance brick
facade and into the lavish interior. Much of the castle was
reconstructed in 1860, with the normal Victorian flair. The
English guidebook is unnecessary, since many rooms have a
handy English information sheet and there are often tours
upon which to freeload. Listen for hymns on the old carillon
at the top of each hour. The many historic paintings are a
fascinating scrapbook of Danish history. Savor the courtyard.
Picnic in the moat park, or enjoy the elegant Slotsherrens
Kro cafeteria at the moat's edge (30 kr, daily summer 10:00-
17:00; April and October 10:00-16:00; November-March
11:00-15:00). Easy parking. From Copenhagen, take the S-
train to Hillerod and then enjoy a pleasant 15-minute walk,
or catch bus #701 or #703 (free with S-tog ticket or train
pass) from the train station (tel. 42 26 04 39).

Louisiana

This is Scandinavia's most raved about modern art museum.
Located in the town of Humlebaek, beautifully situated on the
coast 20 miles north of Copenhagen, Louisiana is a holistic
place—masterfully mixing its art, architecture, and landscape.
Wander from famous Chagalls and Picassos to more obscure
art. Poets spend days here nourishing their creative souls with
new angles, ideas, and perspectives. The views over one of the
busiest passages in the nautical world are nearly as inspiring as
the art. The cafeteria (indoor/outdoor) is reasonable and welcomes picnickers who buy a drink (45 kr admission or included in a special round-trip tour's ticket, daily 10:00-17:00,
Wednesday until 22:00, tel. 42 19 07 19).

Take the train from Copenhagen toward Helsingor,
and get off (in 36 minutes) at Humlebaek. Then it's a free

bus connection (#388) or a 10-minute walk through the woods. From Frederiksborg, there are rare Humlebaek buses, but most will have to connect via Helsingor.

Helsingor

Often confused with its Swedish sister, Helsingborg, just 2 miles across the channel, Helsingor is a small, pleasant Danish town with a medieval center, Kronborg Castle, and lots of Swedes who come over for lower-priced alcohol. There's a fine beachfront hostel, **Vandrerhjem Villa Moltke** (tel. 49 21 16 40), a mile north of the castle. I've met people who prefer small towns and small prices, touring Copenhagen with this hostel as their base (Helsingor TI, tel. 49 70 47 47, two 30-min trains/hr to Copenhagen).

Sights—Helsingor

▲▲**Kronborg Castle**—Helsingor's Kronborg Castle (also called Elsinore) is famous for its questionable (but profitable) ties to Shakespeare. Most of the "Hamlet" castle you'll see today, darling of every big bus tour and travelogue, was built long after Hamlet died, and Shakespeare never saw the place. There was a castle here in Hamlet's day, however, and there was a troupe of English actors working here in Shakespeare's time (Shakespeare may have known them or even been one of them). "To see or not to see?" It's most impressive from the outside.

If you're heading to Sweden, Kalmar Castle (see the chapter on South Sweden) is a better medieval castle. But you're here, and if you like castles, see Kronborg. Don't miss the 20-minute dungeon tours that leave on the half hour. There are English explanations printed in the royal apartments. (20 kr, daily May-September 10:30-17:00; April and October 11:00-16:00; November and March 11:00-15:00; closed Monday off-season, tel. 49 21 30 78.) The grounds (between the walls and sea) are free and great for a picnic, offering a pleasant view of the busy strait separating Denmark and Sweden. If you're rushed, the view from the ferry is as close as you need to get.

Transportation Connections

The above sights are a breeze from Copenhagen by public transportation (see specifics within sights above). Consider getting a Copenhagen Card, which covers your transportation and admission to all major sights.

Route Tips for Drivers

Copenhagen/North Zeeland sights/Helsingor/ Vaxjo, Sweden: Copenhagen to Hillerod (45 min) to Helsingor (30 minutes) to Vaxjo (3½ hours including ferry). Just follow the town name signs. Leave Copenhagen following signs for E-4 and Helsingor. The freeway is great. Hillerod signs lead to the Frederiksborg Castle (not to be confused with the nearby Fredensborg slot, or palace) in the pleasant town of Hillerod. Follow signs to Hillerod C (for center), then "slot" (for castle). While the shortest distance between any two points is the autobahn (E-4 in this case), the "Strand" coastal road (152) is pleasant, going by some of Denmark's finest mansions (including that of Danish writer Karen Blixen, a.k.a. Isak Dinesen of *Out of Africa* fame, in Rungstedlund, which is now a museum).

The freeway leads right onto the ferry to Sweden (follow the signs to Helsingborg, Sweden). Boats leave every 20 minutes. Buy your ticket as you roll on board (310 kr one-way for car, driver and up to five passengers; Thursday, Friday and Saturday 400 kr; round-trip gives you the return at half price). Reservations are free and smart (tel. 33 14 88 80 and wait out the obnoxious tune). If you arrive before your time, you can probably drive onto any ferry.

The 30-minute Helsingor-Helsingborg ferry ride gives you just enough time to enjoy the view of the Kronborg "Hamlet" castle, be impressed by how narrow this very strategic channel is, and change money. The ferry exchange desk's rate is a tad below the banks, but its 5 kr per check fee beats Sweden's standard 40 kr minimum fee for traveler's checks. In Helsingborg, follow signs for E-4 and Stockholm. The road's good, traffic's light, and towns are all clearly signposted. You can change money at the post office in the pleasant town of Markaryd's (just off the road, open late). At Ljungby, road 25 takes you to Vaxjo and Kalmar. Entering Vaxjo, skip the first Vaxjo exit and follow the freeway into "centrum" where it ends. It's about a 6-hour drive from Copenhagen to Kalmar.

CENTRAL DENMARK: AERO AND ODENSE

The sleepy isle of Aero is the cuddle after the climax. It's the perfect time-passed world in which to wind down, enjoy the seagulls, and take a day off. Get Aero-dynamic and pedal a rented bike into the essence of Denmark. Lunch in a traditional kro country inn. Settle into a cobbled world of sailors, who, after someone connected a steam engine to a propeller, decided maybe building ships in bottles is more their style.

On your way to (or from) Aero, drop by the bustling city of Odense, home of Hans Christian Andersen and a fine open-air folk museum.

Planning Your Time

Odense is a transportation hub, the center of the island of Funen. It is an easy stop, worth half a day, on the way to Aero. Aero, more out of the way, is a well-worthwhile headache to get to. Once there, you'll want two nights and a day to properly enjoy it.

Island of Aero

This small (22-by-6-mile) island on the south edge of Denmark is salty and sleepy as can be. Tombstones here say things like, "Here lies Christian Hansen at anchor with his wife. He'll not weigh until he stands before God." It's the kind of island where baskets of new potatoes sit in front of houses—for sale on the honor system. Being about 10 miles across the water from Germany, you'll see plenty of smug Germans who return regularly to this peaceful retreat.

Aeroskobing

Aeroskobing is Aero's town in a bottle. The government, recognizing the value of this amazingly preserved little town, prohibits modern building anywhere in the center. It's the only town in Denmark protected in this way. Drop into the 1680s, when Aeroskobing was the wealthy homeport of over a hundred windjammers. The many Danes, who come here for the tranquillity—washing up the cobbled main drag in

Central Denmark: Aero and Odense

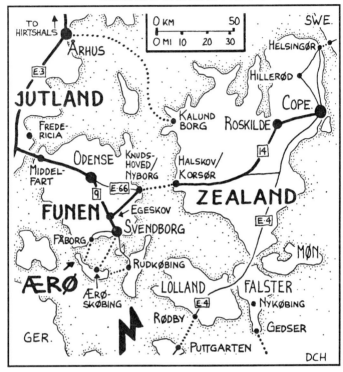

waves with the landing of each boat—call it the fairy tale town. The Danish word for cozy is *hyggelig* (hew-glee), and that describes Aero well.

It's just a pleasant place to wander. Stubby little port-hole-type houses lean on each other like drunk but sleeping sailors, and cast-iron gaslights still shine each evening. The harbor now caters to holiday yachts and on midnight low tides you can almost hear the crabs playing cards. Snoop around. It's okay. Notice all the "snooping mirrors" on the houses. Antique locals may be following your every move. The town economy, once rich with the windjammer trade, hit the rocks in the 20th century. Outside of tourism, there are few jobs. The kids 15-18 years old go to a boarding school in Svendborg. Few return. It's an interesting discussion: do the island folk pickle their culture in tourism or forget about the cuteness and get modern?

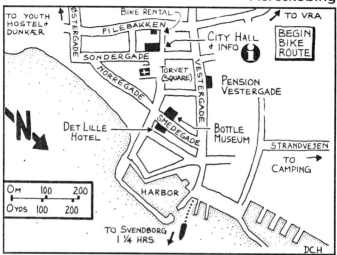

Aeroskobing

Orientation

The town of Aeroskobing is tiny: everything is just a few cobbles from the ferry landing.

Tourist Information

The TI is several blocks up from the ferry on Torvet (Monday-Saturday 9:00-17:00, shorter hours off-season, tel. 62 52 13 00, fax 62 52 14 36). They can find you a 200 kr double in a private home.

Ferries

If you're driving, plan ahead. When you arrive in Aero, reserve a spot on the ferry for your departure (tel. 62 52 10 18).

Sights—Aeroskobing

▲**The "Bottle Peter" Museum** on Smedegade is a fascinating house of 750 different bottled ships. Old Peter Jacobsen bragged that he drank the contents of each bottle except those containing milk. He died in 1960 (most likely buried in a glass coffin), leaving a lifetime of tedious little creations for visitors to marvel at (10 kr, daily 9:00-17:00 May-September, 10:00-16:00 otherwise).

▲**The Hammerich House** is 12 funky rooms in three houses
filled with 200- to 300-year-old junk (15 kr, summer 9:00-16:00,
closed off-season). The third sight in town, the Aero museum,
is nowhere near as interesting as the Hammerich House.

Aero Island Bike Route

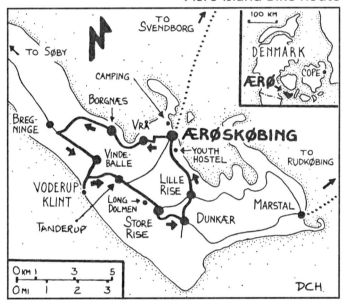

▲▲▲**The Aero Island Bike Ride (or Car Tour)**—This
18-mile trip will show you the best of this windmill-covered
island's charms. While the highest point on the island is
only 180 feet, the wind can be strong and the hills seem
long. This ride is good exercise. If your hotel can't loan you
a bike (ask), rent one from the Energi Station (Pilebaekken
7, tel. 62 52 11 10, go through the green door to the right
of the TI, past the garden to the next road; ask for their free
"cykel map," 35 kr for one-speeds, 40 kr for three-speeds—
about the best 5 kr you could spend on this island). The
youth hostel and the campground also rent bikes. On Aero
there are no deposits and few locks. If you leave in the
morning, you'll hit the Dunkaer Kro Inn in time for lunch.
Ready to go? May the wind be always at your back.

Leave Aeroskobing to the west on the road to Vra.

You'll see the first of many U-shaped farms, typical of this island. The three sides block the wind and are used for storing cows, hay, and people. *Gaard* (farm) shows up on many local names. Until the old generation's gone, you'll see only sturdy old women behind the wheelbarrows. Bike along the coast in the protection of the dyke that made the once-salty swampland to your left farmable. You'll see a sleek modern windmill, and soon, a pleasant cluster of mostly modern summer cottages called Borgnaes. (At this point, wimps can take a shortcut directly to Vindeballe.)

Keep to the right, toward O. Bregninge Mark, pass another Vindeballe turnoff, go along a secluded beach, and then climb uphill over the island's 180-foot summit to Bregninge. Unless you're tired of thatched and half-timbered cottages, turn right and roll through Denmark's "second longest village" to the church. Take a peek inside. (Great pulpit for frustrated preachers and photo hams, public WC in the church yard.) Then roll back through Bregninge past many more U-shaped *gaards*, heading about a mile down the main road to Vindeballe, taking the Voderup turnoff to the right.

A straight road leads you downhill (with a jog to the right) to a rugged bluff called Voderup Klint. If I were a pagan, I'd worship here—the sea, the wind, the chilling view. Notice how the land slipped in long chunks to make terraces stepping down to the sea. Hike down to the foamy beach. While the wind can drag a kite-flier at the top, the beach can be ideal for sunbathing.

Then it's on to Tranderup. You'll roll past the old farm full of cows, a lovely pond, and right past a row of wind-bent stumps. (Care to guess the direction of the prevailing wind?) Follow the sign to Tranderup, stay parallel to the big road through the town, past a lovely farm that does bed and breakfast, the potato stand, and finally to the main road. Turn right. At the Aeroskobing turnoff, just before the tiny little white house, turn left to the big stone (commemorating the return of the island to Denmark from Germany in 1750). Seattle-ites should be sure to visit Claus Clausen's rock (in the picnic area), a memorial to an extremely obscure Washington state pioneer.

Return to the big road, pass the little white house, and head toward Store Rise, the next church spire in the distance.

Just after the Stokkeby turnoff, follow the very rough tree-lined path on your right to the Tingstedet Long Dolmen, just behind the church spire. Here, you'll see a 5,000-year-old early Neolithic burial place, often guarded by the megalithic lamb. Aero had over a hundred of these prehistoric tombs, but few survive.

Carry on down the lane to the Store Rise church. Inside, notice the little ships hanging in the nave, the fine altarpiece, and Martin Luther keeping his Protestant hand on the rudder in the stern. Can you find anyone buried in the graveyard whose name doesn't end in *sen*? Continue down the main road with the impressive—and hopeful—forest of modern windmills on your right until you get to Dunkaer.

Hungry? The newly restored Kro (country inn) serves reasonably priced lunches. And there's a fine little bakery just down the Marstal road.

For the home stretch, take the small road, signed Lille Rise, past the topless windmill. Except for the Lille Rise, it's all downhill from here as you coast past great sea views back home to Aeroskobing.

Still rolling? Bike out past the campground, along the strand (beach) to poke into the coziest little beach houses you'll never see back in the "big is beautiful" U.S.A. This is Europe, where the concept of sustainability is neither new nor subversive.

Sleeping in Aeroskobing
(7 kr = about $1)
Sleep code: **S**=Single, **D**=Double/Twin, **T**=Triple, **Q**=Quad, **B**=Bath/Shower, **WC**=Toilet, **CC**=Credit Card (Visa, Mastercard, Amex).

Pension Vestergade—Phyllis Packness runs this pleasantly quirky old place (built for a sea captain's daughter in 1784) located right on the main street in the town center. She takes very good care of her guests, with a homey TV room and a library with Aero guidebooks you can use. (D-225 kr, D-260 kr with a kitchen, breakfast is extra, good discount for 3-night stays, Vestergade 44, 5970 Aeroskobing, tel. 62 52 22 98.) Loft rooms have great views, climb upstairs to snoop around. This is your ideal home on Aero. Picnic in the backyard or upstairs. Phyllis' pension fills up early, so call well in advance and reconfirm a day or two ahead of arrival.

Det Lille Hotel—This former 19th-century captain's home is warm, tidy, and modern, like a sailboat. A room (S-280 kr, D-395 kr, 120 kr per extra bed) includes a huge breakfast. Just one street off the harbor, next to the cutest house in town (Smedegade 33, 5970 Aeroskobing, tel. 62 52 23 00).

For a budget room in a private home in town, try **Margit Krose** (speaks English, tel. 62 52 24 70) or the **Hoffmann home** (no English spoken, tel. 62 52 12 31). There are several very peaceful bed and breakfasts in the countryside. **Julie and Aksel Hansen's Graasten B&B** is a kid-friendly dairy farm 300 meters from the sea (D-200 kr, cheaper off-season, 35 kr for breakfast, 75 kr evening meals, bike rentals, rooms with kitchenettes, Ostermarksvej 20, 7 km from Aeroskobing towards Marshall, tel./fax 62 52 24 25).

The Aeroskobing Youth Hostel is a glorious place, equipped with a fine living room, a members' kitchen, and family rooms with 2 or 4 beds (70 kr each). The place is usually full mid-June to mid-August and closed October-March. It's 500 yards out of town (Smedevejen 13, tel. 62 52 10 44).

Camping—The three-star campground (follow the waterfront to the left as you face the water, a short walk from the center) is on a fine beach, has a lodge with a fireplace, windsurfing, and cottages for four people for 70 kr, plus 36 kr per person, or 95 kr more with a kitchenette (sheets and blankets rent for 10 kr per day). It's open May-September and always has room for campers at 36 kr each (tel. 62 52 18 54).

Eating in Aeroskobing

Okay, the truth is that without tourism, this island has no economy. The eateries are touristic. Only picnicking is cheap. But good values do hide out. My favorite places are on or near the top of Vestergade (near Pension Vestergade). **Pilegarden** (top Vestergade) and **Phonix** (at the bottom of Vestergade) serve good, reasonably priced food. **Det Lille Hotel** serves a good and reasonable "*dagens ret.*" **Madam Bla's Coffeehouse** (Vestergade 39) is more expensive, with delicious candle-lit-cuddly or garden-cheery meals. **MUMM**'s candle-lit ambience is occasionally blown out by the German yachting crowd, but the food is fine and reasonably priced (Sondergade 12). A $4

dinner? The **bakery** next to the Bog Café serves homemade
bread, cheese, a tin of liver paste, and a liter of drinkable
yogurt. The homemade waffle cones in the pink shop across
the street from the Vestergade Pension are stomping good.

Transportation Connections

Aero and Odense: The Svendborg-Aeroskobing ferry is a
pleasant 70-minute crossing (255 kr round-trip per car and
driver, 85 kr round-trip per person, you can leave via any of
the three different Aero ferries). There are five boats a day
(7:30, 10:45, 14:30, 17:30, and 21:00, Saturday and Sunday
morning departures about an hour later, but double check),
and while walk-ons always make it on board, cars need reservations (tel. 62 52 10 18). A special ferry/bus combo ticket
gives you the whole island with stop-overs.

Grahundbus goes regularly from Copenhagen to Aero (180
kr). Call 44 68 44 00 and ask about bus #862 "Vandbussen."

Odense

Founded in 988, named after Odin, the Nordic Zeus, and
important economically only in the 19th century when a
canal enabled it to become the port city of the garden
island's produce, Odense is famous today primarily for its
hometown storyteller, Hans Christian Andersen. Andersen
once said, "Perhaps Odense will one day become famous
because of me, and perhaps people from many countries will
travel to Odense because of me." Today, Odense (OH-then-
za) is one of Denmark's most visited towns. Denmark's
third-largest city, with 170,000 people, it is big and industrial. But its old center retains some of the fairy-tale charm
it had in the days of H.C.A., and has plenty to offer.

The TI, in the town hall right downtown (open daily
summer 9:00-19:00, Sunday 11:00-19:00; off-season
Monday-Friday 9:00-17:00, Saturday 10:00-13:00, tel. 66
12 75 20), runs city bus tours and a Meet the Danes program. For a quick visit, all you need is the free map/guide
from the Hans Christian Andersen Hus.

Sights—Odense

▲**The Funen Village Open-Air Museum** is a sleepy
gathering of 24 old buildings preserving the 18th-century

culture of this region. There are no explanations in the buildings, because the many school groups who visit play guessing games. Pick up the 15 kr guidebook. (20 kr admission, open daily June-August 10:00-19:30; April-May and September-October 10:00-16:00. tel. 66 13 13 72.) From mid-July to mid-August, there are H. C. Andersen plays in the theater at 16:00 every afternoon. The 45 kr play ticket includes admission 90 minutes early (not before 14:30) to see the museum.

▲▲**Hans Christian Andersen Hus**—This museum is packed with mementos from the popular writer's life, his many letters and books, and hordes of children and tourists. It's fun if you like his tales. (20 kr admission, open daily summer 9:00-18:00, shorter hours off-season, Hans Jensensstraede 39.) Things are explained well in English, so the guidebook is unnecessary (but pick up the free city guide). The garden fairy tale parade (with kid-pleasing HCA play vignettes) thrills kids daily in the museum garden at 11:00, 13:00, and 15:00. Across the street is a popular shop full of imaginative mobiles and Danish arts and crafts. Just around the corner is Flensted Uromagerens Hus (the mobile-makers' house).

▲**Montergarden Urban History Museum**—Very close to the H.C.A. Hus (15 kr, near the H.C.A. Hotel, daily 10:00-16:00), this fun little museum offers three stories of Odense history, early photos, a great coin collection, and the cheapest coffee in Denmark (3 kr).

Sleeping in Odense
(7 kr = about $1)
The H.C.A. Hotel has a special July to mid-August deal (650 kr doubles, with breakfast, tel. 66 14 78 00) for those who'd like to spend the night.

Transportation Connections
Odense to: Copenhagen (hrly, 3 hrs, train goes right onto the ferry), **Arhus** (hrly, 2 hrs), **Svendborg** (hrly, 1 hr, to Aero ferry), **Roskilde** (hrly, 2½ hrs).

Route Tips for Drivers
Arhus or Billund to Aero: The freeway takes you over a suspension bridge on the island of Fyn (Funen in English).

At Odense take Highway 9 south to Svendborg. Ideally, call the day before to confirm ferry times. If you're taking your car, get a reservation. Figure about 2 hours to drive from Billund to Svendborg.

Leave your car in Svendborg (at the easy long-term parking lot 2 blocks from the ferry dock) and sail for the cast-away isle of Aero. The Svendborg-Aeroskobing ferry is a pleasant 70-minute crossing (255 kr round-trip per car and driver, 85 kr round-trip per person). There are only five boats a day (7:30, 10:45, 14:30, 17:30, and 21:00; Saturday and Sunday morning departures about an hour later, but double check), and while walk-ons always make it on board, cars need reservations (tel. 62 52 10 18). A special ferry/bus combo ticket gives you the whole island with stop-overs.

Aero-Copenhagen via Odense: Catch the 6:00 ferry back to Svendborg (7:00 Saturday and Sunday). Call 62 52 10 18 for information. Reservations for walk-ons are never necessary. On Saturday and Sunday, there are normally no early trips. By 7:40, you'll be driving north on Highway 9; follow signs first to Faborg, past the Egeskov castle to Odense. If you're doing the folk museum, leave Route 9 just south of town at Hojby, turning left toward Dalum and the Odense Campground (on Odensveg). Look for Den Fynske Landsby signs (near the train tracks, south edge of town). If you're going directly to fairytaleland, drive into town and follow the signs to H. C. Andersen Hus. Parking is simple on the street near the H. C. Andersen Hotel (set your window clock, 1-hr limit). Drop into the hotel to get the free, excellent Odense map/guide (you can also get it at the HCA Hus). Everything's dead until 9:00. There's coffee in the hotel, or buy your picnic on Overgade street.

It's a 30-minute drive from Odense to the ferry (following signs for Nyborg, E-20 and Knudshoved). The freeway passes Nyborg and butts right up to the Knudshoved-Halsskov ferry. Call 33 14 88 80, 53 75 15 77, or 65 31 40 54 for a free reservation, but they're rarely necessary, and tickets cost 270 kr for a car, driver, and up to four passengers each way. Boats leave about twice an hour for the 1-hour crossing. In a few years, the bridge that you see next to the ferry will be finished (and so will the ferry company). It will end halfway across the strait with a tunnel that spirals straight down and does the rest of the crossing underground. On Zealand, head for Copenhagen. At Ringsted, signs will take you to Roskilde. Set your sights on the twin church-spires and then follow signs to Vikingskibene, the Viking ships.

Copenhagen is just 30 minutes from Roskilde. If you're returning your car to the airport, stay on E-20 to the bitter end, following signs to Kobenhavn C, and then to Dragor/Kastrup Airport.

JUTLAND: LEGOLAND AND ARHUS

Jutland, the part of Denmark that juts up from Germany, is a land of sand dunes, Lego toys, moated manor houses, and fortified old towns. Make a pilgrimage to the most famous land in all of Jutland: the pint-sized kid's paradise, Legoland. In Arhus, the lively capital of Jutland, wander the pedestrian street of this busy port, tour its boggy pre-history, and visit centuries-old Danish town life in its open-air museum.

Planning Your Time

Jutland is worth two days on a three-week trip through Scandinavia. On a quick trip, drivers coming in from Norway might take the overnight boat from Kristiansand to Hirtshals. By noon you'll be in Arhus. The Gen Gamle By (old town museum) is worth an afternoon. Spend the next morning at Legoland, on the way to Funen and Aero. Speedier travelers could make Arhus an afternoon stop only and drive to Lego land that evening (which is free if you enter late).

Legoland

Legoland is Scandinavia's top kids' sight. If you have one (or think you might be one), it's a fun stop. This huge park is a happy combination of rides, restaurants, trees, smiles, and 33 million Lego bricks creatively arranged into such wonders as Mt. Rushmore, the Parthenon, "Mad" Ludwig's castle, and the Statue of Liberty. It's a Lego world here, as everything is cleverly related to this very popular toy. Surprisingly, however, the restaurants don't serve Legolamb.

The indoor "museum" features the history of the company, high-tech Lego creations, a great doll collection, and a toy museum full of mechanical wonders from the early 1900s, many ready to jump into action as soon as you push the button. There's a Lego playroom for hands-on fun—and a campground across the street if your kids refuse to move on. (Open daily May to mid-September 10:00 to 20:00; until 21:00 in July; closed off-season, 95 kr entry, 80 kr for kids age 3-13, 60 kr for kids over 60; gets you on all the rides, if

Jutland: Legoland and Arhus

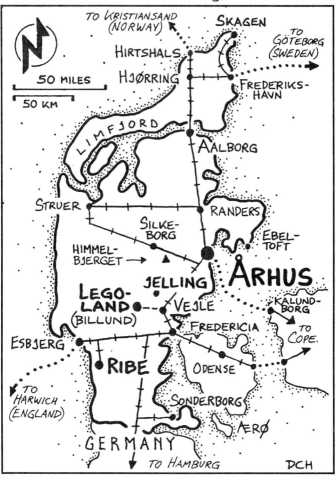

you arrive after 17:30, 18:30 July and early August, tel. 75 33 13 33). The gates are unguarded, but don't worry, Legoland doesn't charge in the evening. Some rides close down a little early, but it's basically the same place after dinner as during the day—with fewer tour groups.

Legoland is located in the otherwise unremarkable town of Billund. The local tourist office (in Legoland, tel. 75 33 19 26) can arrange rooms. (See Sleeping and Connections, below.)

Sights—Near Legoland

Jelling—I know you've always wanted to see the hometown of the ancient Danish kings, Gorm the Old and Harold Bluetooth. And this is your chance. Jelling is a small village (12 miles from Legoland, just off the highway near Vejle) with a small church that has Denmark's oldest frescoes and two old runic stones in its courtyard—often called "Denmark's birth certificate."

▲Ribe—A Viking port a thousand years ago, Ribe is the oldest, and possibly loveliest, town in Denmark. It's an entertaining mix of cobbled lanes and leaning old houses with a fine church (5 kr, bright modern paintings under old Romanesque arches). A smoky, low-ceilinged, very atmospheric inn, the Weis Stue, rents a few rooms and serves good meals across the street from the church (tel. 75 42 07 00). Drop by the TI for its handy walking tour brochure, or better yet, catch one of the guided town walks (20 kr, daily 11:30, Torvet 3, tel. 75 42 15 00).

Sleeping in Billund
(7 kr = about $1)

Billund is near Legoland. Sleep code: **S**=Single, **D**=Double/Twin, **T**=Triple, **Q**=Quad, **B**=Bath/Shower, **WC**=Toilet, **CC**=Credit Card (**V**isa, **M**astercard, **A**mex).

The **Legoland Hotel** adjoins Legoland (825 kr for a family-of-four room including discounted admission to the park, tel. 75 33 12 44).

Private rooms are the key to a budget visit here. The following three places are great, with about four doubles, and a cheaper 4- to 6-bed hut for campers with sleeping bags. Each has a kitchenette, pleasant family rooms, a kid-friendly yard, Legos to play with, and discounts for children. The first two are very close to the park; the woman at the third speaks the best English.

Eva and Egon Jorgensen (D-250 kr, 30 kr for a fancy but small breakfast, Koldingvej 1, tel. 75 33 10 46). This one is the easiest to find: as you're entering Billund on road 28, turn left where the sign says "Legoland to the right." Drive past the large Lego factory (and giant Legos) and take the first driveway on the right at the flags and "Room" sign.

Anna and Victor Christensen house visitors just a long block behind the Legoland parking lot (D-225 kr, 30 kr breakfast, big garden, TV in room, Systemvej 25, Billund, tel. 75 33 15 68).

Mary Sort has a great setup in a forest just outside of town. Her guests enjoy a huge living room, lots of Lego toys, and a kitchen (D-260 kr including breakfast, leave Billund on the Grindsted road, turn right on Stilbjergvei after Shell station, about a half-mile down the road on the right at Stilbjergvei 4, tel. 75 33 23 27).

Billund Youth Hostel is brand new with 85 kr dorm beds and D-275 kr (Ellehammers Alle 12, 7190 Billund, tel. 75 33 19 26, fax 75 33 28 77, the bus from Vejle stops right there).

Arhus

Denmark's second-largest city, with a population of 260,000, Arhus (oar-hoos) is Jutland's capital and cultural hub. Its Viking founders, ever conscious of aesthetics, chose a lovely wooded where-the-river-hits-the-sea setting. Today, it

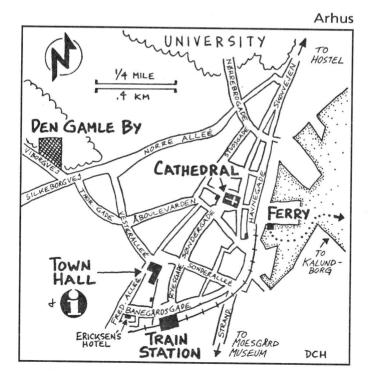

Arhus

bustles with a lively port and an important university. It's well worth a stop.

Tourist Information
Visit the TI in the town hall (open daily 9:00-20:00, mid-June to mid-September; until 16:30 and closed Sunday other months, tel. 86 12 16 00, fax 86 12 08 07) to get the helpful Arhus brochure and map. They run a fine city introductory bus tour (daily in summer at 10:00 for 2½ hours from the TI; 45 kr which also gives you 24 hours of unlimited city bus travel). City buses easily connect the center and train station with the open air and prehistory museums.

Sights—Arhus
▲▲▲**Den Gamle By**—The Old Town open-air folk museum puts Arhus on the touristic map. This is a unique gathering of seventy half-timbered houses and crafts shops, all wonderfully furnished just like back in the days of Hans Christian Andersen. The Mayor's House (from 1597) is the nucleus, and reason enough to visit. Unlike other Scandinavian open-air museums, which focus on rural folk life, Den Gamle By re-creates old Danish town life. (40 kr entry, open daily June-August 9:00-18:00; May and September 9:00-17:00; shorter hours off-season; ask about walking tours often at 13:00 and 16:00, there are some English descriptions inside, pick up the schedule of tours; take bus #3 or walk 15 minutes from the train station to the Old Town, tel. 86 12 31 88.) After hours, the buildings are locked, but the peaceful park is open. There's a fine botanical garden next door.

▲**Forhistorisk Museum Moesgard**—This prehistory museum at Moesgard, just south of Arhus, is famous for its incredibly well-preserved Grauballe Man. This 2,000-year-old "bog man" looks like a fellow half his age. You'll see his skin, nails, hair, and even the slit in his throat given him at the sacrificial banquet. The museum has fine Stone, Bronze, Iron, and Viking Age exhibits. (25 kr, open daily 10:00-17:00; off-season 12:00-16:00, closed Monday.) Take bus #6 from the Arhus station to the last stop. Behind the museum, a prehistoric open-air museum ("trackway") stretches 2 miles down to a fine beach (good 10 kr guidebooklet) where, in the summer, bus #19 takes you back downtown. The museum cafeteria sells picnics-to-go if you're in the mood.

Arhus Cathedral—This late Gothic (from 1479) church is Denmark's biggest—over 300 feet long and tall (open daily except Sunday 9:30-16:00; shorter hours off-season).

Other Arhus Attractions—Arhus has a great pedestrian street that stretches at least two ice cream cones from the cathedral to the train station (Sondergade/Clements Torv). There's lots more to see and do in Arhus, including an art museum, a Viking museum (free, in a bank basement across from the cathedral), and a "Tivoli" amusement park.

Sleeping in Arhus
(7 kr = about $1)
All accommodations are centrally located near the train station and TI. Sleep code: **S**=Single, **D**=Double/Twin, **T**=Triple, **Q**=Quad, **B**=Bath/Shower, **WC**=Toilet, **CC**=Credit Card (Visa, Mastercard, Amex).

Missionshotellet Ansgar is a huge traditional hotel (D-500 kr-600 kr with breakfast, 14 Banegardsplads, tel. 86 12 41 22, fax 86 20 29 04).

Ericksen's Hotel is a shipshape, friendly, creative little place with showers down the hall, and cheap meals (D-400 kr, plus 35 kr for breakfast, Banegardsgate 6-8, tel. 86 13 62 96, fax 86 13 76 76).

The Arhus city **Sleep In** is an alternative culture center offering 75 kr dorm beds, cheap meals, and rental blankets (open 24 hours a day, mid-June to mid-September, Havgate 20, tel. 86 19 20 55; confirm its existence with the TI before walking there).

The TI can set you up in a private home for 110 kr per person. They also have summer deals on ritzy hotels that can match the prices of the two hotel listings above. The local **Youth Hotel** is a good one, with plenty of family rooms, situated near the water 2 miles out of town on Ostreskovvej, tel. 86 16 98 72, bus #1, #6, #9, or #16 to the end and follow the signs.

Eating in Arhus
The pizza at **Restaurant Italia** (corner of Mindebrogade and Aboulevarden) is popular and reasonable. **Munkestuen** has

good 100 kr meals (Klostertorvet 5, tel. 86 12 95 67). The park in front of Musikhuset concert hall is good for picnics.

Transportation Connections
Arhus to: Hirtshals (16/day, 2½ hrs), **Odense** (16/day, 2 hr), **Copenhagen** (hrly, 4½ hrs), **Hamburg** (3/day, 5½ hrs).

Day and night, **ferries** sail between Hirtshals, Denmark, and Kristiansand, Norway. On board, you'll find a decent smorgasbord, music, duty-free shopping, and a bank (no fee). The crossing takes just 4 hours (overnight, 6) and the cost ranges wildly from 84 kr-338 kr. (July and weekends are priciest). The charge for a car is 210 kr; a "car package" deal lets five in a car travel for 1,020 kr (summer, Monday-Thursday). On the overnight crossing, you can sleep in varying levels of comfort and privacy (35 kr for a reclining seat, 85 kr for a couchette, 120 kr for a bed in a 4-berth room, or 170 kr for a bed in a private double with shower). Call Color Line for information, schedules, and reservations (tel. 00-47-38 07 88 88). You can phone in a reservation (advisable if you've got a car or want to rent a room) and pay when you arrive at the dock.

Route Tips for Drivers
Ferry dock at Hirtshals to Arhus to Billund: From the dock in Hirtshals, drive E-45 south (signs to Hjorring, Aalborg). It's about a 2-hour drive even if you take the more scenic road 507 from Alborg (signs to Hadsund). E-45 brings you right into central Arhus. Those skipping Arhus will skirt the center, turning right on Nordre Ringgade to follow E-45 south. To get to the Arhus commercial center, follow signs to the center, then Domkirke. There's a handy pay parking lot right across from the cathedral. You'll see signs all over town directing you to the open-air folk museum, Den Gamle By.

From Arhus continue south on E-45 (leave on the Skanderborg road, signs to Vejle, Kolding). For Legoland, take the Velje S (after the Velje N) exit sign Billund. Billund is a non-threatening Lego-sized town.

OSLO

Oslo is the smallest and least earthshaking of the Nordic capitals, but this brisk little city offers more sightseeing thrills than you might expect. Sights of the Viking spirit—past and present—tell an exciting story. Prowl through the remains of ancient Viking ships and marvel at more peaceful but equally gutsy modern boats like the *Kon Tiki*, *Ra*, and *Fram*. Dive into the country's folk culture at the Norwegian Open Air Folk Museum and get stirred up by the country's heroic spirit at the Norwegian Resistance Museum.

For a look at modern Oslo, browse through the new yuppie-style harbor shopping complex, tour the recently avant garde city hall, take a peek at sculptor Vigeland's people pillars, and climb the towering, knee-shaking Holmenkollen ski jump.

Situated at the head of a 60-mile-long fjord, surrounded by forests, and 500,000 people, small Oslo is Norway's cultural hub and an all-you-can-see smorgasbord of historic sights, trees, art, and Nordic fun.

Planning Your Time

Oslo offers an exciting two-day slate of sightseeing thrills. Ideally, sleep on the train in from Stockholm, spend two days, and leave on the night train to Copenhagen, or on the scenic train to Bergen the third morning. Spend the two days like this:

Day 1: Set up. Tour the Akershus Castle and Nazi Resistance museum. Take a picnic on the ferry to Bygdoy and enjoy a view of the city harbor. Tour the Fram, Kon Tiki, and Viking Ships. Finish the afternoon at the Norwegian Open Air Folk museum. Boat home. For evening culture consider the Norwegian Masters performance (18:00) and the Folk music and dance show (21:00 Monday and Thursday).

Day 2: At 10:00 catch the City Hall tour, then browse through the National museum. Spend the afternoon at Vigeland Park, and at the Holmenkollen ski jump and museum. Browse Karl Johans Gate (all the way to the station)

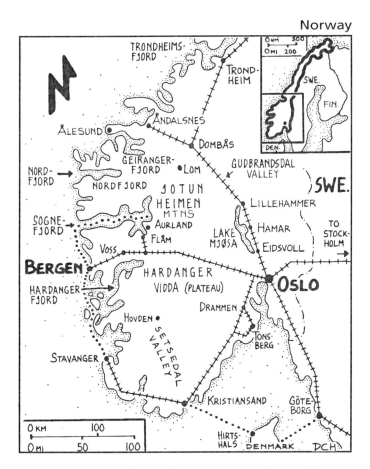

and Aker Brygge harbor in the early evening for the Norwegian paseo. Consider munching a fast food dinner on the mini-harbor cruise.

Orientation

Oslo is easy to manage, with nearly all its sights clustered around the central "barbell" (Karl Johans Street with the Royal Palace on one end and the train station on the other), or in the Bygdoy district, a 10-minute ferry ride across the harbor.

Tourist Information

The **Norwegian Information Center** (on the waterfront next to the city hall, daily 9:00-20:00, shorter hours off season, tel. 22 83 00 50) displays Norway as if it was a giant booth at a trade show. Stock up on brochures for Oslo and all of your Norwegian destinations, especially the Bergen guide. Pick up the free Oslo map, Sporveiskart transit map, *What's on in Oslo* monthly (for the most accurate listing of museum hours and special events), *Streetwise* magazine (hip and fun to read, telling you how to definitely not be one of those tourists), the free annual Oslo Guide, and consider buying the Oslo Card (see below). They have a rack of free pages on contemporary Norwegian issues and life (near the door), a 30-minute "multi-vision" show taking you around Norway (free, top of the hour, in a theater in the back), and rooms showcasing various crafts and ways you can spend your money here. The tourist information window in the central station (daily 8:00-23:00, less off-season, tel. 22 17 11 24) is much simpler, but can handle all of your needs just as well.

Use It is a hardworking youth information center, providing lots of solid money-saving, experience-enhancing information to young, student, and vagabond travelers (summer only 7:30-18:00, Saturday 9:00-14:00, closed Sunday, Mollergata 3, tel. 22 41 51 32). Read their free *Streetwise* magazine for ideas on eating and sleeping cheap, good night spots, best beaches, and so on.

The **Oslo Card** (24 hours–110 kr, 48 hours–190 kr, or 72 hours–240 kr) gives you free use of all city public transit, boats, free entry to all sights, a free harbor "mini cruise" tour, free parking, many more discounts, and a handy handbook. As admissions go up, this card becomes an increasingly better deal. Almost any 2-day visit to Oslo will be cheaper with the Oslo Card (which costs less than three Bygdoy museum admissions, the Ski Jump, and one city bus ride). The TI's special Oslo Package hotel deal (described under Sleeping, below) includes this card with your discounted hotel room.

Because of Norway's passion for minor differences in opening times from month to month, I've generally listed only the peak season hours. Assume opening hours shorten as the days do. The high season in Oslo is mid-June to August. (I'll call that "summer" in this chapter.)

Getting Into and Around Oslo

Trains

The central train station is slick and helpful, with a late-hours TI, room-finding service, late-hours bank (fair rates, normal fee), supermarket (daily 7:00-23:00), and an **Interrail Center** (open 7:00-23:00, mid-June to September, offering any traveler with a train pass, 10 kr showers, free rucksack storage racks, a bright and clean lounge, cheap snacks, a bulletin board for cheap sleeping deals, and an information center; train info tel 22 17 14 00, 7:00-23:00).

Public Transportation

Oslo's public transit system is made up of buses, trams, ferries, and a subway. Tickets cost 16 kr and are good for 1 hour of use on any combination of the above. (Flexi-cards give 10 for 130 kr, buy tickets as you board, bus info tel. 177.) The **Trafikanten**, the public transit information center, is under the ugly tower immediately in front of the station. Their free Sporveiskart transit map is the best city map around and makes the transit system quite inviting. Use it. The *"Tourist Ticket"* is a 35 kr 24-hour transit pass that pays for itself on the third ride. The Oslo Card (see Tourist Information, above) gives you free run of the entire transit system. Note how gracefully the subway lines fan out after huddling at Stortinget. Take advantage of the way they run like clockwork with schedules clearly posted and followed.

Bike Rental

Oslo is a good biking town, especially if you'd like to get out into the woods or ride a tram uphill out of town and coast for miles back. Den Rustne Eike ("the rusty spoke" on the harbor next to the Norway Information Center, daily May-September 10:00-18:30, tel. 22 83 72 31) rents bikes (3 hrs/60 kr, 6 hrs/80 kr) organizes tours.

Sights—Downtown Oslo

▲▲**City Hall**—Construction on Oslo's richly decorated Radhuset began in 1931. It was finished in 1950 to celebrate the city's 900th birthday. Norway's leading artists all

Oslo Center

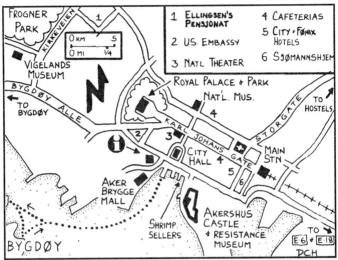

contributed to what was an avant garde thrill in its day.
The interior's 2,000 square yards of bold and colorful
murals (which take you on a voyage through the collec-
tive psyche of Norway, from its simple rural beginnings
through the scar tissue of the Nazi occupation and beyond)
are meaningful only with the excellent, free guided tours
(15 kr, 10:00, 12:00 and 14:00 Monday-Friday, entry on
the Karl Johans side; open 9:00-15:30, Sunday 12:00-
15:00, tel. 22 86 16 00).

▲**Akershus Castle**—One of the oldest buildings in town,
this castle overlooking Oslo's harbor is mediocre by European standards, but worth a look if you're there for the tour.
Its grounds make a pleasant park with grassy ramparts,
pigeon-roost cannons, and great picnic spots with city views
(English tours, free, daily summer at 11:00, 13:00 and 15:00,
Sunday 13:00 and 15:00 only; 50 minutes long, open daily
10:00-16:00, Sunday 12:30-16:00; May to mid-September,
closed in winter, 15 kr, tel. 22 41 25 21).

▲▲**Norwegian Resistance Museum (Norges
Hjemmefront-museum)**—A stirring story about the Nazi
invasion and occupation is told with wonderful English
descriptions. This is the best look in Europe at how national
spirit can endure total German occupation (in the Akershus

Castle, 15 kr, daily summer 10:00-17:00, Sunday 11:00-17:00, closes 1 hour earlier off-season).

▲**National Gallery**—Located downtown (13 Universitets Gata), this easy-to-handle museum gives you an effortless tour back in time and through Norway's most beautiful valleys, mountains, and villages with the help of its romantic painters (especially Dahl). It also has a noteworthy impressionist collection, some Vigeland statues, and a representative roomful of Munch paintings, including one of two *Screams*. The Munch paintings here make a trip to the Munch museum unnecessary for most (free, Monday, Wednesday, Friday, and Saturday 10:00-16:00; Thursday 10:00-20:00; Sunday 11:00-15:00, closed Tuesday, tel. 22 20 04 04).

▲▲**Browsing**—Oslo's pulse is best felt along and near the central Karl Johans Gate (from station to palace) and in the trendy new harborside Aker Brygge Festival Market Mall (a glass-and-chrome collection of sharp cafés and polished produce stalls just west of the city hall). The buskers are among the best in Europe.

▲▲▲**Vigeland Sculptures in Frogner Park and the Vigeland Museum**—The 75-acre park contains a lifetime of work by Norway's greatest sculptor, Gustav Vigeland. From 1906 through 1942, he sculpted 175 bronze and granite statues. The statues—all nude and each unique—surround Vigeland's 60-foot-high tangled tower of 121 bodies called "the monolith of life." Pick up the free map from the box on the kiosk wall as you enter. The park is more than great art. It's a city at play. Enjoy its urban Norwegian ambience. Then visit the Vigeland Museum to see the models for the statues and more in the artist's studio. Don't miss the photos on the wall showing the construction of the monolith (museum open 10:00-18:00, Sunday 12:00-19:00, closed Monday, 20 kr, open 12:00-16:00 and free off-season, tel. 22 44 11 36). The park is always open and free. Take T-banen #2 or bus #72, #73, or #20 to Frogner Plass.

Oslo City Museum—Located in the Frogner Manor farm in the Frogner park, this museum tells the story of Oslo since 1909. A helpful free English brochure guides you through the exhibits (20 kr, open 10:00-18:00, Saturday and Sunday 11:00-17:00, closed Monday; shorter hours off-season, tel. 22 43 06 45).

▲▲**Edvard Munch Museum**—The only Norwegian painter to have a serious impact on European art, Munch (monk) is a surprise to many who visit this fine museum. The emotional, disturbing, and powerfully expressionist work of this strange and perplexing man is arranged chronologically. You'll see paintings, drawings, lithographs, and photographs. Don't miss *The Scream*, which captures the fright many feel as the human "race" does just that (50 kr, 10:00-18:00, Sunday 12:00-18:00, off-season closed at 16:00 and all day Monday, tel. 22 67 37 74). If the price or location is a problem, you can see a roomful of Munch in the free National Gallery downtown.

Sights—Oslo's Bygdoy Neighborhood

▲▲▲**Bygdoy**—This exciting cluster of sights is on a park-like peninsula just across the harbor from downtown (reached by bus #30 from the Station and National Theater or by ferry, departing from City Hall three times an hour, 8:30-21:00, 16 kr, free with transit pass or Oslo card). The Folk Museum and Viking ships are near the first stop, Dronningen. The other museums are at the second stop, Bygdoynes. (See inset on the Greater Oslo map.) Otherwise, all Bygdoy sights are within a 15-minute walk of each other.

▲▲**Norwegian Folk Museum**—Brought from all corners of Norway, 140 buildings are reassembled on these 35 acres. While Stockholm's Skansen claims to be the first (and was the first to open to the public), this museum is a bit older, starting in 1885 as the king's private collection. You'll find craftspeople doing their traditional things, security guards disguised in cute, colorful, and traditional local costumes, endless creative ways to make do in a primitive log-cabin-and-goats-on-the-roof age, a 12th-century stave church, and a museum filled with toys and fine folk costumes. The place hops in the summer but is dead off-season. Catch the free 1-hour guided walks (call for schedule). Otherwise, glean information from the 20 kr guidebook and the informative guards who look like Rebecca Boone's Norwegian pen-pals (50 kr, daily June-August 10:00-18:00; off-season 11:00-17:00). For folk-dance performances, tour, and crafts demonstration schedules, call 22 43 70 20.

▲▲**Viking Ships**—Three great ninth-century Viking ships are surrounded by artifacts from the days of rape, pillage,

Greater Oslo

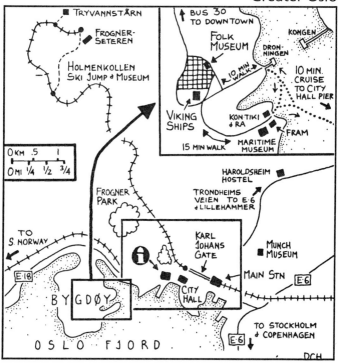

and—ya sure ya betcha—plunder. Don't miss the old cloth and embroidery in the dark room you light by entering. There are no museum tours, but everything is well described in English, and it's hard not to hear the English-speaking bus tour guides. There was a time when much of a frightened Europe closed every prayer with "and deliver us from the Vikings, Amen." Gazing up at the prow of one of these sleek time-stained vessels, you can almost hear the screams and smell the armpits of those redheads on the rampage (20 kr, daily summer 9:00-18:00, less in off-season).

▲▲The *Fram*—This great ship took modern-day Vikings Amundsen and Nansen deep into the Arctic and Antarctic, farther north and south than any ship before. For three years the *Fram* was part of an arctic ice drift. The exhibit is fascinating. Read the ground floor displays, then explore the boat (20 kr, daily summer 9:00-17:45, shorter hours off-season). You can step into the lobby and see the ship's hull for free. Dry-docked by the waterfront is the boat Amundsen used to "discover" the northwest passage (Fram ticket gets you aboard).

▲▲The *Kon Tiki* **Museum**—Next to the *Fram* are the *Kon Tiki* and the *Ra II*, the boats Thor Heyerdahl built and sailed 4,000 and 3,000 miles, respectively, to prove that early South Americans could have sailed to Polynesia and Africans could have populated Barbados. He made enough money from his adventures to also prove that rich Norwegians can stay that way only by moving to low-tax Monaco (25 kr, daily 9:00-18:00, off-season 10:30-17:00).

▲**Norwegian Maritime Museum**—If you like the sea, this museum is a saltlick, providing a fine look at Norway's maritime heritage (20 kr, daily 10:00-19:00, off-season 10:30-16:00).

Other Oslo Sights and Activities

▲**Henie-Onstad Art Center** Norway's best private modern art collection, donated by the famous Norwegian Olympic skater/movie star, Sonja Henie (and her husband), combines modern art, a stunning building, a beautiful fjord-side setting, and a great café/restaurant. Don't miss Sonja Henie's glittering trophy room near the entrance. (30 kr, Monday, Saturday, and Sunday 11:00-17:00; Tuesday-Friday 9:00-21:00; in Hovikodden, tel. 67 54 30 50, 8 miles SW of Oslo, bus #151, #153, #161, #162, #251, or #261 from the main station.)

▲▲**Holmenkollen Ski Jump and Ski Museum**— Overlooking Oslo is a tremendous ski jump with a unique museum of skiing. The T-bane gets you out of the city and into the hills and forests that surround Oslo. After touring the history of skiing in the museum, ride the elevator and climb the 100-step stairway to the thrilling top of the jump for the best possible view of Oslo—and a chance to look down the long and frightening ramp that has sent so many tumbling into the agony of defeat. The ski museum is a must for skiers—tracing the evolution of the sport from 4,000-year-old rock paintings to crude 1,500-year-old skis to the slick and quickly evolving skis of our century. (Ski Jump and Museum open daily 9:00/10:00-22:00 in July; till 20:00 June and August; closes earlier off-season, 50 kr.)

For a special thrill, step into the **Simulator** and fly down the French Alps in a Disneyland-style downhill ski race simulator. My legs were exhausted after the 4-minute terror. This stimulator, parked in front of the ski museum, costs 35 kr. (Japanese tourists, who wig out over this one, are usually given a free ride after paying for four.)

To get to the ski jump, ride the T-bana (tram 15) to the Holmenkollen stop and hike up. For a longer but easier walk, ride to the end of the line and walk down past the Frognerseteren Hovedrestaurant. This classy, traditional old place, with a terrace that offers a commanding view of the city, is a popular stop for apple cake and coffee or a splurge dinner (open until 22:00, tel. 22 14 37 36).

The nearby Tryvannstarnet observatory tower offers a lofty 360-degree view with Oslo in the distance, the fjord and endless forests, lakes, and soft hills. It's impressive, but not necessary if you climbed the ski jump, which gives you a much better view of Oslo.

Forests, Lakes, and Beaches—Oslo is surrounded by a vast forest dotted with idyllic little lakes, huts, joggers, bikers, and sun-worshippers. Mountain bike riding possibilities are endless (as you'll discover if you go exploring without a guide or good map). For a quick ride, you can take the T-banen (with your bike, it needs a ticket too) to the end of line #15 (Frognerseteren, 30 minutes from Nationaltheatret, gaining you the most altitude possible) and follow the gravelly roads (mostly downhill but with some climbing) past several dreamy lakes to Sognsvann at the end of T-banen line #4 (a 1-hr ride, not counting time lost). Farther east, from Maridalsvannet, a bike path follows the Aker River all the way back into town. For plenty of trees and none of the exercise, ride the T-banen to Sognsvann (with a beach towel rather than a bike) and join in the lake-side scene. Other popular beaches (like those on islands in the harbor) are described in Use It's *Streetwise* magazine.

Harbor and Fjord Tours—Several tour boats leave regularly from Pier 3 in front of the city hall. A relaxing and scenic 50-minute mini-cruise with a boring three-language commentary departs hourly and costs only 60 kr (or free with Oslo Card, daily 10:00-20:00, tel. 22 20 07 15). They won't scream if you bring something to Munch. The cheapest way to enjoy the scenic Oslo fjord is to simply ride the ferries which regularly connect the nearby islands with downtown (free with the city transport pass).

▲▲▲**Folk Entertainment**—A group of amateur musicians and dancers (Leikarringen, Bondeungdomslaget) gives a short, sweet, caring, and vibrant 1-hour show at the Oslo Concert Hall (100 kr, 60 kr for students, Monday and Thursday in July and August at 21:00; tel. 22 83 32 00, look for the big brown glassy overpass on Munkedamsveien, the recommended Vegata Vertshus restaurant is just up the street). For their off-season concert schedule (different locales, usually once a week), call 22 41 40 70.

▲**Grieg, Ibsen, and Munch: Norwegian Masters**—For an evening of Norwegian classical music (Grieg), poetry (Ibsen), and art (Munch) in the elegant 150-year-old Gamle Logen concert hall, consider this concert. A cast of four including a pianist, violinist and soprano explore how the collage of nature and life unique to Norway inspired the masters. This is accomplished by weaving their words, music, and paintings into a 70-minute drama (160 kr, almost nightly in summer at 18:00, Kirkegaten behind the Akershus Fort, all in English, tel. 22 43 43 70). Get there early enough to prepare for the performance by reading the program. (This is heavy-duty culture—husbands should down a Coke or coffee beforehand.) For 70 minutes, it's a bit pricey. But from cow-calls to Trollhaugen to the *Scream*, (other than reading the rest of my books) this is your most accessible opportunity to gain an appreciation of the creative Norwegian mind.

Parks, Pools, and Wet Fun—The Tusenfryd Amusement Park offers over fifty rides, plenty of entertainment, family fun, and restaurants. A free, hourly coach shuttles fun-seekers 20 minutes to the park from the Oslo City Hall (50 kr, 60 kr in July, free with Oslo Card, open 10:30-20:00, 22:00 in July).

Oslo offers lots of water fun for about 35 kr. In Frogner Park, the Frognerbadet (mid-May to August, Middelthuns-gate 28, tel. 22 44 74 29, free with Oslo card) has a sauna, outdoor pools, lots of young families, a cafeteria, and high dives. Toyenbadet is a modern indoor pool complex with mini golf and a 100-yard-long water slide (free with Oslo Card, open at odd hours throughout the year, Helgengate 90, a 10-minute walk from Munch Museum, tel. 22 67 18 89). Oslo's botanical gardens (free) are nearby. (For more ideas on swimming, see *Streetwise*.)

Nightlife—They used to tell people who asked about night-life in Oslo that Copenhagen was only an hour away by air-plane. Now Oslo has sprouted a nightlife of its own. The scene is always changing. The tourist office has information on Oslo's many cafés, discos, and jazz clubs. Use It is the best source of information for local hot spots.

Shopping—For a great selection (but high prices) in sweaters and other Norwegian crafts, shop at Husfliden (daily 9:00-17:00, Saturday until 14:00, Den Norske Husflidsforening, 4 Mollergate behind the cathedral, tel. 22 42 10 75), the retail center for the Norwegian Association of Home Arts and Crafts. Shops are generally open 10:00-18:00. Many stay open until 20:00 on Thursday and close early on Saturday and all day Sunday.

Sleeping in Oslo
(7 kr = about $1)

Yes, Oslo is expensive. In Oslo, the season dictates the best deals. In low season (July to mid-August, and Friday, Satur-day and Sunday the rest of the year) fancy hotels are the best value for softies with 600 kr for a double with breakfast. In high season (business days outside of summer), your afford-able choices are dumpy-for-Scandinavia (but still nice by European standards) hotel doubles (300 kr-400 kr) and 270 kr doubles in private homes. For experience and economy (but not convenience), go for a private home. Oslo's two hostels are far from the center, expensive (160 kr per bed), and usually full. Summer vagabonds sleep cheap (100 kr) at the downtown sleep-in.

Like its sister Scandinavian capitals, Oslo's hotels are designed for business travelers. Expensive in high season, empty otherwise. Only the TI can sort through all the con-fusing hotel "specials" and get you the best deal possible on a fancy hotel—push-list rooms at about half price. Half price is still 500 kr-600 kr, but that includes breakfast and a lot of extra comfort for a few extra kroner over the cost of a cheap hotel. Cheap hotels, whose rates are the same throughout the year, are a bad value in summer, but offer a real savings in low season. The TI's "Experience Oslo" package adver-tises 600 kr doubles in business-class (1,200 kr) rooms and includes a free Oslo Card (worth 100 kr/day).

Only use the TI for these push-list deals, not for cheap hotels or private homes. Many of the cheapest hotels (my listings) tell the TI (which gets a 10% fee) they're full when they're not. Go direct. A hotel getting 100 percent of your payment is more likely to have a room. July and early August are easy, but early June and September can be tight.

Sleep code: **S**=Single, **D**=Double/Twin, **T**=Triple, **Q**=Quad, **B**=Bath/Shower, **WC**=Toilet, **CC**=Credit Card (**V**isa, **M**astercard, **A**mex).

Sleeping in Hotels near the Train Station

Each of these places is within a 2-minute walk of the station, in a neighborhood your mom probably wouldn't want you hanging around in at night. The hotels themselves, however, are secure and comfortable. Leave nothing in your car. The Paleet parking garage is handy but not cheap—120 kr per 24 hours.

Sjomannshjem (S-250 kr-300 kr, simple seventh-floor D-300 kr, sixth-floor D/DWCB-400 kr with newer furniture, no breakfast, elevator; enter on Fred Olsengate, Tollbugt 4, 0152 Oslo, tel. 22 41 20 05) is a "retired seaman's hotel." But since most Norwegian captains are commanding Third World sailors these days, the seaman's union welcomes tourists in their underused Oslo hotel. One of Oslo's great bargains, it's plain, clean, simple (e.g., one towel for your entire stay), and shipshape.

City Hotel, clean, basic, very homey, and with a wonderful lounge, originated 100 years ago as a cheap place for Norwegians to sleep while they waited to sail to their new homes in America. It now serves the opposite purpose. (DBWC-500 kr-800 kr depending on season, with breakfast, CC:VMA, Skippergatan 19, tel. 22 41 36 10, fax 22 42 24 29.)

Rainbow Hotel Astoria (SWCB-375 kr-585 kr, TwinWCB-500 kr-685 kr, DWCB-600 kr-785 kr, with buffet breakfast, rates vary with season, CC:VMA, 3 blocks in front of the station, 50 yards off Karl Johans Gate, Dronningensgate 21, 0154 Oslo, tel. 22 42 00 10, fax 22 42 57 65) is a comfortable, modern place, part of the quickly growing "Rainbow Hotels" chain which understands what comforts are worth paying for. There are smoke-free floors, an included buffet breakfast, televisions, telephones, full modern bathrooms in each room. Ice machines! Most "twins" are actually "combi" rooms with a regular bed and a fold down sofa bed.

The newest Oslo Rainbow hotel is **Rainbow Hotel Spectrum** ("combi" TwinBWC-500 kr-685 kr, full doubles 100 kr more, no smoking rooms available, 3 blocks to the right as you leave the station on Lilletorget, Brugata 7, 0186 Oslo, tel. 22 17 60 30, fax 22 17 60 80) is also well located and a good value.

Sleeping in the West End

Ellingsen's Pensjonat, run by a friendly woman whose name is Mrs. Wecking (Viking), is a textbook example of a good accommodations value with no lounge or breakfasts, dreary halls but fine rooms, fluffy down comforters, and a great residential location 4 blocks behind the Royal Palace (a lot of S-190 kr, 3 D-300 kr, call well in advance for doubles, Holtegt 25, 0355, Oslo 3, on the corner of Uranienborg veien and Holtegatan, near the Uranienborg church, it's the #25 on the east side of the street, T-banen #1 from the station, tel. 22 60 03 59, fax 22 60 99 21).

Cochs Pensjonat (D-380 kr, DBWC-490 kr, no breakfast, CC:VM, tram #11 to Parkveien 25, tel. 22 60 48 36, fax 22 46 54 02) has plain rooms and a stale wet-noodle atmosphere, but is right behind the palace.

Lindes Pensionat is a great deal with kitchenette and refrigerator (D-270 kr for 2 or more nights, no breakfast, near Frogner park, train #2 to Frogner Plass, 41 Thomas Heftyes Gate, tel. 22 55 37 82).

Sleeping in Private Homes

The Caspari family rents three comfortable rooms in their home (S-150 kr, D-270 kr without breakfast, price with book if you go direct, one shared bathroom, extra cots available for 100 kr, 60 kr extra for 1-night stay, a 15-minute walk from the center, behind Frogner park, immediately across the street from the Heggeli T-bana stop at Heggeliveien 55, same side you exit train on, tel. 22 14 57 70). This woodsy, peaceful suburb is a place you'd like to raise your kids in—or call home for a couple of days in Oslo. And it couldn't be handier by T-banen, literally a few steps and 7 minutes from the center.

Mr. Naess (S-125 kr, D-250 kr, T-375 kr, 40 kr extra for one night, no breakfast, walk 20 minutes from the station or take bus #27 or #56 from tower in front of station 5 stops to Olaf Ryes Place, facing a park at Toftestrasse 45, tel. 22 37 58 94) offers big, homey old rooms overlooking a park and the use of a fully-loaded kitchen. More urban, this place is a flat in a big old building with plenty of work-a-day shops and eateries nearby.

Sleeping in Youth Hostels

Haraldsheim Youth Hostel (IYHF), a huge, modern hostel, is open all year, situated far from the center on a hill with a grand view, laundry, and self-service kitchen. Its 270 beds (4 per room) are often completely booked. Beds in the new fancy quads with private showers and toilets are 165 kr per person with buffet breakfast. (Simpler beds cost 145 kr, with breakfast, sheets 35 kr, guest membership 25 kr, 4 Heraldsheimveien, tram #1 or #7 from station to Sinsen, 4 km out of town, 5-minute uphill hike.) Eurailers can train (2/hr, to Gressen) to the hostel for free (tel. 22 15 50 43).

Holtekilen Sommerhotel is a comfortable university dorm a bit out of town (June to mid-August, D-390 kr with breakfast, 145 kr dorm beds with breakfast, sheets 35 kr, non-members 25 kr extra, Michelets vei 55, Stabekk/Oslo 1320, train to Stabbek and walk 10 minutes, or bus #151 or #251 and walk 3 minutes, ideal for drivers, go west 9 km from center, exit E-18 at Strand, tel. 67 53 38 53).

YMCA Sleep-In Oslo—Located near the station, this sleep-in offers the cheapest mattresses in town in three large unisex rooms with 30 mattresses each, left luggage room, piano lounge, kitchen, and ear plugs for sale. It's as pleasant as a sleep-in can be (100 kr, no bedding provided, you must bring a sleeping bag, open 8:00-11:00, 17:00-24:00 July to mid-August, Mollergata 1, entry from Grubbegata, one block beyond the cathedral, tel. 22 20 83 97). They take no reservations, but call to see if there's a place.

Sleeping on the Train

Norway's trains offer 100 kr beds in triple compartments. Eurailers who sleep well to the rhythm of the rails have several very scenic overnight trips to choose from (it's light until midnight at Oslo's latitude for much of the early summer).

Eating in Oslo

The thought of a simple open-face sandwich (which looks and tastes like half of something I can make, with an inedible garnish added) for $5, and a beer for nearly as much, ruins my appetite. Nevertheless, one can't continue to sightsee on postcards and train tickets alone.

My strategy is to splurge for a hotel that includes breakfast. A 50 kr Norwegian breakfast is fit for a Viking. Have a picnic for lunch or dinner. There are plenty of grocery stores. Big department stores have huge first-class supermarkets in their basements with lots of picnic dinner-quality alternatives to sandwiches. Most of the little yogurt tubs with cereal come with a collapsible spoon. The train station has a late hours grocery.

Since Norwegians eat early, between 16:00-19:00, the cheapest places close by 19:00. Later dinners are elegant dining and normally quite expensive. Pizzerias and salad bars are the trend. Ask your receptionist for advice. Many pizzerias have all-you-can-eat specials. Chinese and ethnic places are everywhere and reasonably priced.

The **Aker Brygge** (harborfront mall) development isn't cheap, but it has some cheery cafés, classy delis, open-till-22:00 restaurants, and markets. The **Cruise Café** has reasonable light meals.

Oslo's several **Kaffistova** cafeterias are alcohol-free, clean (check out the revolving toilet seats), and serve simple, hearty, and typically Norwegian (read "bland") meals for the best price around. At 8 Rosenkrantzgate, you'll get your choice of an entrée and all the salad, cooked vegetables, and "flat bread" you want (or at least need) for around 80 kr. It's open 12:00-21:00 (17:00 Saturday, 18:00 Sunday) in summer and closes earlier off-season. The **Norrona Cafeteria** is another traditional budget-saver (65 kr *dagens ratt*, central at 19 Grensen, closes at 17:00, 19:00 off-season). Other cafeterias are found in department stores.

Vegeta Vertshus, which has been keeping Oslo vegetarians fat, happy, and low on the food chain for fifty years, serves a huge selection of hearty vegetarian food that would satisfy even a Republican president. Fill your plate once (medium plate/65 kr, large plate/75 kr) or eternally for 98 kr. How's your balance? One plate did me fine (daily 10:00-

23:00, no smoking, no alcohol, no meat, Munkedamsveien 3B, near top of Stortingsgata between palace and city hall, tel. 22 83 42 32).

Transportation Connections

Oslo to Bergen: These cities are linked by a spectacularly scenic 7-hour train ride. Reservations are required. Departures are at about 7:30, 10:30, 15:30, 15:40, and 23:00 daily in both directions (480 kr, or 380 kr if you buy a day early and don't travel on Friday or Sunday). For more info, see "The Oslo-Bergen Train" in chapter on Fjords, Mountains, and Valleys.

Oslo to Copenhagen: Consider the cheap quickie cruise that leaves daily from Copenhagen (departs 17:00, returns 9:15 2 days later; 16 hrs sailing each way and 7 hrs in Norway's capital). See Copenhagen chapter for specifics.

FJORDS, MOUNTAINS, AND VALLEYS

While Oslo and Bergen are the big touristic draws, Norway is essentially a land of natural beauty. While there is a certain mystique about the "land of the midnight sun," you'll get the most scenic travel thrills per mile, minute, and dollar by going west rather than north.

Leave Oslo and meander across the center of the country along an arc of tradition-steeped valleys, myth-inspiring mountains, and troll-thrilling fjords. This chapter describes two ways to cover Norway's greatest natural charms:

1. A series of dramatic train, boat, and bus rides called "Norway in a Nutshell," which is done easily in a day from or between Oslo and Bergen.

2. For those with a car and a little more time, the powerfully scenic arc up Gudbrandsdalen Valley, over the Jotunheim mountains, and down and along Norway's greatest fjord, Sognefjord. Both routes do the great Aurlandsfjord branch of Sognefjord.

Fjord Country and Norway in a Nutshell

Norway's greatest claim to scenic fame is her deep and lush fjords. A series of well-organized and spectacular bus, train, and ferry connections, appropriately called "Norway in a Nutshell," lays Norway's most beautiful fjord country spread-eagle on a scenic platter. This is the seductive Sognefjord—tiny but tough ferries, towering narrow canyons, and isolated farms and villages marinated in the mist of countless waterfalls. You're an eager Lilliputian on the Norwegian Gulliver of nature.

Today, the region enjoys very mild weather for its latitude thanks to the warm Gulf Stream. But 3 million years ago, an ice age made this land as inhabitable as the center of Greenland. Like the hairline on Dick Clark, the ice slowly receded. As the last glaciers of the Ice Age cut their way to the sea, they grooved out long troughs—today's fjords. Since the ice was thicker inland and only a relatively thin lip at the coast, the gouging was deeper inland. The average fjord is 4,000 feet deep far inland and only around 600 feet deep where it reaches the open sea.

Fjords, Mountains, and Valleys

The entire west coast is slashed by stunning fjords, but the Sognefjord, Norway's longest (120 miles) and deepest (over a mile), is tops. Anything but Sognefjord is, at best, foreplay. This is it, the ultimate natural thrill Norway has to offer. Aurland is a good home base for your exploration. Aurlandsfjord, a remote, scenic, and accessible arm of the Sognefjord, is possibly the juiciest bite in the scenic pomegranate of Norway. The local weather is actually decent, with about 24 inches of rain per year, compared to over 6 feet annually in nearby Bergen.

Planning Your Time

Even the blitz tourist needs a day for the "Norway in a Nutshell" trip. This is easily done as a long day trip from Oslo. (All connections are designed for the tourists, explained in English, and are convenient and easy.) Ideally, break the trip with an overnight in Aurland, carry on into Bergen, and enjoy a day in Bergen before sleeping on the night train (past all the scenery you saw westbound) back to Oslo. Those with a car and only one day should take the train from Oslo. With more time, drivers can improve on the "nutshell" by following the more time-consuming and thorough version of this scenic smorgasbord explained in the second half of this chapter.

Norway in a Nutshell

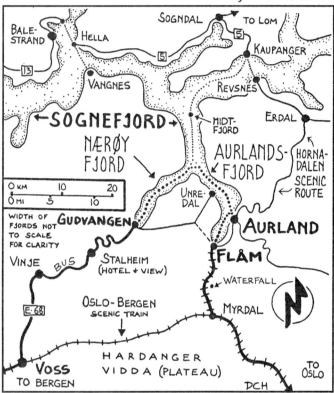

Sights—Norway in a Nutshell

The most exciting single day trip you could make from Oslo or Bergen is this circular train/boat/bus/train trip through this spectacular chunk of fjord country. Rushed travelers zip in and out by train from Oslo or Bergen. Those with more time do the "nutshell" segments at their leisure. It's famous, everybody does it, and if you're looking for the scenic grandeur of Norway, so should you.

The all-day trip starts by train every morning from Oslo and Bergen. Tourist offices have brochures with exact times. It's a good side trip or an exciting way to connect the two cities. Here's the route in a nutshell: ride the Oslo-Bergen train to Myrdal, take the scenic Myrdal-Flam train, hop on the Flam-Gudvangen cruise, and then take the Gudvangen-Voss bus. (It's easy. Just follow the crowds.) At Voss, jump on the Oslo-Bergen train, and head west for Bergen or east for Oslo. The sights and segments are described below.

▲▲**The Oslo-Bergen Train**—This is simply the most spectacular train ride in northern Europe. You'll hang out the window with your camera smoking as you roar over Norway's mountainous spine. The barren, windswept heaths, glaciers, deep forests, countless lakes, and a few rugged ski resorts create a harsh beauty. The railway, an amazing engineering feat completed in 1909, is 300 miles long, peaks at 4,266 feet (which at this Alaskan latitude is far above the tree line) goes under 18 miles of snow sheds, over 300 bridges, and through 200 tunnels in just under 7 hours. (About 500 kr, 100 kr cheaper if you buy a day early and don't travel on Friday or Sunday, departures at about 7:30, 10:30, 15:30, 15:40, and 23:00 daily in both directions, reservations required.) Nutshell travelers get off the Oslo-Bergen train at Myrdal and rejoin it later.

▲▲**Myrdal-Flam Train**—This little 12-mile spur line leaves the Oslo-Bergen line at Myrdal (2,800 feet) and winds down to Flam (sea level) in 50 thrilling minutes. It's party time on board and the conductor even stops the train for photos at the best waterfall. This line has twenty tunnels (over 3 miles' worth) and is so steep that the train has five separate braking systems. You can hike down to Flam (4 hrs, great mountain scenery but no fjord views) or hike the best 2 hours from Myrdal to Berekvam where you can catch the train into the valley. Myrdal is nothing but a scenic train junction.

▲**Flam**—On the Norway-in-a-Nutshell route, this scenic, touristy town at the head of the Aurlandsfjord is little more than a train station, ferry landing, and cluster of hotels and hostels. (TI tel. 57 63 21 06, daily June-September 8:30-20:30, then shorter hours.) For accommodations, see Sleeping, below.

▲▲**Aurland**—A few miles north of Flam, Aurland is more of a town and less of a tourist depot. Nothing exciting, but it's a good easygoing fjord-side home base (see Sleeping, below). You can hike up the valley or tour the electrical works (public tours show visitors the source of most of Oslo's electricity from July to mid-August, Monday-Friday at 12:00 and 13:30, tel. 57 63 32 92). The harborside public library is a pleasant refuge, and the 800-year-old church is worth a look.

The area has as many goats as people (1,900). The one who runs the tourist office (mid-June to August, 9:00-19:00, Saturday and Sunday 10:00-16:00, shorter hours off-season, pick up the English-language Bergen guide) speaks English (tel. 57 63 33 13). The local *geitost* (goat's cheese) is sweet and delicious. Note: Every train (except for the late-night one) arriving in Flam connects with a bus to Aurland. Fifteen buses and at least four ferries connect the towns daily. The nearest bike rental is at the Flam TI.

▲▲▲**Flam/Aurland-Gudvangen Fjord Cruise**—At Flam, if you're doing the Nutshell Suite, follow the crowds and hop on the sightseeing boat. (Boats leave Flam daily at 9:00, 10:35, 14:05, and 14:30, each stopping at Aurland, then continuing to Gudvangen, 120 kr one-way, 60 kr for those with a train pass or ISIC card, couples ask for the "family" discount which lets the spouse go for half price.) The boat takes you right into the mist of the many fjord waterfalls, and close to the goats, sheep, and awesome cliffs.

You'll cruise up the lovely Aurlandsfjord and hang a left at the stunning Naeroyfjord. It's a breathtaking voyage. For 90 glorious minutes, camera-clicking tourists scurry on the drool-stained deck like nervous roosters scratching fitfully for a photo to catch the magic. Waterfalls turn the black rock cliffs into a bridal fair, and you can nearly reach out and touch the sheer cliffs of the awesome Naeroyfjord. The ride is the ultimate fjord experience. It's one of those fine times, like when you're high on the tip of an Alp, and a warm camaraderie spontaneously combusts between all the strangers who came together for the experience.

You can request a stopover in Unredal or Stovi (which has a farm museum). There's an idyllic 2-km shore walk

from Stovi. If you get off, you can let the next boat know
that you'd like to be picked up by turning on a signal light.
Gudvangen-Voss Bus—Gudvangen is little more than a
boat dock and giant tourist kiosk. Norway Nutshellers get
off the boat at Gudvangen and catch a bus (50 kr, about a
1-hour ride, buses depart with each ferry landing) up the
Naeroydalen (Narrow Valley) to Voss.

Voss—An ugly town in a lovely lake and mountain setting,
Voss does have an interesting folk museum, a 13th-century
church, and a few other historic sights, but it's basically a
home base for summer or winter sports. At Voss, the bus
drops you at the train station (on the Oslo-Bergen train line,
heading west to Bergen or east to Oslo). Drivers should zip
right through. Because of its location, you may need to
spend the night. (TI tel. 56 51 17 16, **Vang Pensjonat**,
D-460 kr, tel. 56 51 21 45; **Kringsja Pension**, D-480 kr,
DBWC-560 kr, tel. 56 51 16 27; or the luxurious **Voss
Youth Hostel**, tel. 56 51 20 17.)

▲▲**Sognefjord Scenic Express Boat**—Speedy boats run
between Flam and Bergen through the Sognefjord. (Boats
depart Bergen 8:00 and arrive in Flam 13:30, depart Flam
15:30 and arrive in Bergen 20:45, daily in June, July, and
August; all stop in Aurland, 430 kr, or 325 kr with a train
pass or hotel card, 460 kr round-trip special returning
by train).

▲**Unredal**—This almost impossibly remote community of
52 families was accessible only by boat until 1985, when the
road from Flam was opened. Unredal has Norway's smallest still-used church (12th-century). The 15-minute drive
from Flam is mostly through a new tunnel. There's not
much in the town, which is so famous for its goat's cheese
and small church, but I'll never forget the picnic I had on
the ferry wharf. If you want the ferry to stop, turn on the
blinking light. You'll sail by Unredal on the Flam-Gudvangen
boat trip.

Sleeping on Sognefjord
(7 kr = about $1)
Sleep code: **S**=Single, **D**=Double/Twin, **T**=Triple, **Q**=Quad,
B=Bath/Shower, **WC**=Toilet, **CC**=Credit Card (**V**isa,
Mastercard, **A**mex).

Sleeping in Flam

Heimly Lodge is doing its best to go big-time in a small-time town. It's clean, efficient, and the best normal hotel in town. (D-600 kr, DBWC-800 kr with breakfast, CC:VMA, tel. 57 63 23 00, fax 57 63 23 40.) Sit on the porch with new friends and watch the clouds roll down the fjord. Located 400 yards along the harbor from the station.

    Flam Youth Hostel and Camping Bungalows has the cheapest beds in the area. On the river just behind the Flam train station, the Holand family offers dorm beds in 4-bed youth hostel rooms (80 kr per bed with kitchenette, 25 kr for sheets, 25 kr if not a hostel member). They also have some D-275 kr with bedding, 4-bed cabins for 275 kr without sheets, and a deluxe cabin for 500 kr (tel. 57 63 21 21). Note that the season is boom or bust here and it can be very crowded in July and August.

Sleeping in Aurland

Aabelheim Pension, located right in the town center, is run by friendly old Gurid Stigen. This is far and away Aurland's best cozy-like-a-farmhouse place. (Cozy is *koselig*, a good Norwegian word.) Gurid speaks only Norwegian, but she laughs in any language. (6 D-330 kr, breakfast 63 kr, very traditional award-winning living room, mid-June to early September, tel. 57 63 34 49.)

    Vangen Motel, also nestled in downtown Aurland, is a simple old hotel that offers very basic rooms (all with private showers, D-400 kr, or only 325 kr if you provide the sheets). There's a big self-serve kitchen and a dining and living area. Open all year. The motel has 4-bed huts right on the beach for 350 kr without sheets (tel. 57 63 35 80).

    At the farm house **Skahjem Gard**, Aurland's deputy mayor, Nils Tore, rents out family apartments (one 300 kr hut, five 500 kr huts, all with BWC and kitchenettes, tel. 57 63 33 29). It's a 20-minute walk from town, but he will pick up and drop off travelers at the ferry. This is best for families who are driving.

    Aurland Fjord Hotel is a modern place with more comfort and less traditional coziness. Basic restaurant, central location, friendly, with a pub. (DBWC-950 kr with breakfast, CC:VMA, tel. 57 63 35 05, fax 57 63 36 22.)

Up Gudbrandsdalen Valley
to the Mountains of Jotenheim
and down to Sognefjord

This more in-depth look at scenic Norway is best for drivers with more time. Gudbrandsdalen Valley (*dal* means valley, so this is redundant) is the country of Peer Gynt, the Norwegian Huck Finn. This romantic valley of time-worn hills, log cabins, and velvet farms has connected north and south Norway since ancient times. Lillehammer, with Norway's best folk museum, provides an excellent introduction. You might spend the night in a log and sod farmstead-turned-hotel, tucked in a quiet valley under Norway's highest mountains.

Next Norway's highest mountain pass takes you on an exhilarating roller coaster ride through the heart of Jotunheim (the giant's home). Jotunheim bristles with Norway's most gigantic mountains.

The road then hairpins down into fjord country, where a softer world awaits with fjords full of medieval stave churches, peely fishing boats, and brightly painted shiplap villages.

Planning Your Time

While you could enjoyably spend 5 or 6 days in this area, on a 3-week Scandinavian rampage this slice of the region is worth 3 days. I'd spend them like this:

Day 1: Leave Oslo early, spend midday at the Maihaugen Open Air Folk Museum for a tour and picnic. Drive up Gudbrandsdalen Valley with a short stop at the Lom church. Evening in Jotenheim country.

Day 2: Drive out of the mountains, along Lustrafjord, over Hornadalen Pass and into Aurlandsfjord. Sleep in Aurland.

Day 3: Cruise the Aurlands and Naeroy fjords before carrying on to Bergen.

Sights—In the Gudbrandsdalen Valley

▲**Lillehammer**—This pleasant winter and summer resort town of 23,000 was the smallest town ever to host the winter Olympics (1994). Any visit should include the high-tech and Olympics Experience Centre (55 kr, daily 10:00-20:00, Sunday 12:00-20:00, request an English-language showing of the 15-minute eight-projector slide presentation on the upcoming games). The exhibit entry fee includes a ski jump simulator. Lillehammer has a happy old wooden pedestrian zone and several interesting museums, including a popular transportation museum and the Maihaugen Open-Air Folk Museum. Lillehammer's TI (9:00-21:00, less on week-ends and off-season, tel. 61 25 92 99) and the Olympic Information Centre are situated right in the colorful pedestrian shopping zone. The town's best budget hotel is the **Gjestehuset Ersgaard** (D-460 kr, DBWC-590 kr with breakfast, CC:VMA, 2 km east and above town at Nordsetterveien 201, tel. 61 25 06 84, fax 61 25 31 09).

▲▲▲**Maihaugen Open-Air Folk Museum**—Located in Lillehammer, this wonderfully laid out look at the local culture provides a wonderful introduction to the Gudbrandsdalen Valley. Anders Sandvig, a "visionary dentist," started the collection in 1887. The outdoor section has 150 old buildings from the Gudbrandsdalen region with plenty of free English tours, crafts in action, and even people living there from ages ago (Williamsburg-style, July only).

Indoors, the "And slowly the land became our own" exhibit, gives a look at local life during the Ice Age, the Vikings, the plague, the Industrial Revolution, etc. The indoor museum also has the original shops of 40 crafts and tradespeople (such as a hatter, cooper, bookbinder, and Dr. Sandvig's old dental office). There's a thorough English guidebook (50 kr), English descriptions at each house, and free 45-minute guided tours daily in English (11:00, 12:00, 13:00, 15:00 and sometimes on request).

The museum welcomes picnickers and has a café and an outdoor cafeteria (60 kr, 9:00-19:00 June-August, 10:00-16:00 shoulder season, houses are closed in the winter, tel. 61 25 01 35; call to be sure you arrive for a tour, especially outside of summer). Ask on arrival about special events, crafts, or music, and don't miss the indoor museum. Maihaugen is a steep 20-minute walk or short bus ride from the Lillehammer train station.

▲**Eidsvoll Manor**—During the Napoleonic period, Denmark was about to give Norway to Sweden. This ruffled the patriotic feathers of Norway's Thomas Jeffersons and Ben Franklins, and in 1814, Norway's constitution was written and signed in this stately mansion (in the town of

Eidsvoll Verk, north of Oslo). It's full of elegant furnishings and stirring history (2 kr, 10:00-17:00, 12:00-15:00 in shoulder season, tel. 63 95 13 04).

Scenic Drives—Two side trips give visitors a good dose of the wild beauty of this land. Peer Gyntveien is a 30 kr troll road that leaves E-6 at Tretten, looping west for 25 miles and rejoining E-6 at Vinstra. This trip sounds romantic, but it's basically a windy, curvy dirt road over a high desolate heath and scrub brush plateau with fine mountain views: scenic, but so is E-6. The second, lesser known but more rewarding, scenic side trip is the Peer Gynt Seterveg.

▲**Lom**—This isn't much of a town—except for its great stave church, which causes the closest thing to a tour-bus jam this neck of the Norwegian woods will ever see. Drop by the church (you'll see its dark spire just over the bridge, 20 kr, 9:00-21:00, mid-June to mid-August, shorter off-season and during funerals, fine 5 kr leaflet, check out the little footbridge over the waterfall), and take advantage of the tourist information office (9:00-21:00, 12:00-18:00 Sunday in summer, shorter hours off-season, tel. 61 21 12 86). Lom, about 6 miles north of Roisheim, has plenty of accommodations, but I'd sleep elsewhere.

Sights—In the Jotunheim Mountains

▲▲**Sognefjell**—Norway's highest mountain crossing (4,600 feet at the summit) is a thrilling drive through a can-can line of northern Europe's highest mountains. In previous centuries, the farmers of Gudbrandsdalen took their horse caravans over this difficult mountain pass on their necessary treks to Bergen. Today, the road (Route 15), is still narrow, windy, and otherworldly, but usually closed from mid-October-May. The ten hairpin turns between Turtagro and Fortun are white-knuckle exciting. Be sure to stop, get out, and enjoy the lavish views. Treat each turn as if it was your last.

Scenic Drives and Hikes—From the main road near Boverdal and Roisheim, you have several options springing from three toll roads. The Boverdal youth hostel has good information and a fine 1:150,000 hiking map.

Spiterstulen: From Roisheim, this 18-km toll road (30 kr) takes you to the Spiterstulen mountain hotel/lodge (1,600 meters). This is the best destination for serious all-day

hikes to Norway's two mightiest mountains: Glittertinden
(2,470 meters) and Galdhopiggen (a 4-hr hike up and a
3-hr hike down, doable without a guide).

Juvasshytta: This toll road, starting from Boverdal,
takes you the highest you can drive and the closest you can
get to Galdhopiggen by car (1,840 meters). At the end of the
50 kr toll road, there are daily guided 5-hour hikes across the
glacier to the summit and back (10:00 and 11:30 in the summer, 6-km each way, 60 kr, hiking shoes a good idea, easiest
ascent but very dangerous without a guide). You can sleep in
the Juvasshytta lodge (D-400 kr, D without sheets-350 kr,
130 sheetless beds in larger rooms, sheets 20 kr, breakfast
75 kr, dinner 140 kr, tel. 61 21 15 50).

Leirvassbu: This 18-km, 30 kr toll road is most scenic
for "car hikers." It takes you to a lodge (owned by the Hotel
Elvesaeter people, see Sleeping, below) at 1,400 meters with
great views and easy walks. A serious (4-hr round-trip) hike
goes to the lone peak, Kyrkja (2,030 meters).

Besseggen: This ridge offers an incredible opportunity
to hike between two lakes separated by 5 feet of land and a
1,000-foot cliff. To get to the trail head, drivers detour down
road #51 after Otta south to Maurvangen. Turn right to
Gjendsheim to park your car. From Gjendesheim, catch the
boat to Memurubu. The path starts at the boat dock. Hike
along the ridge with a blue lake on one side and a green lake
on the other, and keep your balance. The 6-hour trail leads
back to Gjendesheim. (This is a major detour: Gjendsheim is
about 55 miles from Roisheim.)

▲▲**Jostedalsbre's Nigardsbreen Glacier Hike**—Jostedalsbre is the most accessible branch of mainland Europe's
largest glacier (185 square miles) and the Nigardsbreen
GlacierHike is a good chance for a hands-on glacier experience. It's an easy drive up Jostedal from Lustrafjord.

From Gaupne, drive up road #604 for 23 miles just past
Elvekrok, where you take the private toll road (15 kr) for 2 miles
to the lake. (Look for Breheimsenteret, an information center on
the glacier and its history at the entrance to the Nigard Glacier
valley, May-September, daily in summer 9:00-20:00, tel. 57 68
32 44.) From here take the special boat (two 15-min rides per
hour, 10:00-18:00, mid-June to mid-August, 15 kr round-trip)
to within a 20-minute walk of the glacier itself.

The walk is steep and slippery in places. Follow the red marks. There are 90-minute guided "family" walks of the glacier (60 kr, daily from 12:00 depending on demand, minimum age 5, I'd rate them PG-13 myself, you get clamp-on crampons). Tougher glacier hikes are also offered (240 kr including boots, real crampons, and more, daily 10:30 and 13:00, 4 hrs, but you'll need to be at the Glacier Center nearly 2 hours early to buy tickets and pick up your gear).

Respect the glacier. It's a powerful river of ice, and fatal accidents are not uncommon. The guided walk is the safest, and exciting enough. Use the Gaupne TI (tel. 57 68 15 88) to confirm your plans. If this is your first glacier, it's worth the time and hike even without the tour. If glaciers don't give you tingles and you're feeling pressed, it's not worth the long drive.

Sights—On the Lustrafjord Branch of Songnefjord

Lustrafjord—This arm of the famous Sognefjord is rugged country. Only 2 percent of this land is fit to build or farm on. Lustrafjord is ringed with tiny villages where farmers sell cherries and giant raspberries on the honor system. Urnes, perched on the east bank of Lustrafjord, has an ancient stave church and a less ancient ferry dock (ferries connect with sleepy Solvorn on the west bank, car crossings at the bottom of each hour 10:30-16:30, pedestrian ferries more often, 10-minute ride, 30 kr round-trip).

▲▲**Urnes Stave Church**—A steep, but pleasant, 20-minute walk takes you from the town of Urnes to Norway's oldest stave church (1150) and the most important artistic and historic sight in the region (25 kr, 10:30-17:30, June-August, ask for an English tour).

Sogndal—About a 10-minute drive from the Kaupanger ferry, Sogndal is the only sizable town in this region. It's big enough to have a busy shopping street and a helpful TI (tel. 57 67 30 83). Ten miles east of Sogndal, on the west bank of the Lustrafjord, **Solvorn** is a sleepy little Victorian town. Its tiny fjerry crosses the fjord regularly to Urnes (10-min ride, 32 kr round-trip). See Sleeping, below.

Kaupanger-Gudvangen by Post Boat—Romantic post boats take mail and tourists through an arm and elbow of the

Sognefjord. Marvel at the staggering Naeroyfjord. Boats leave Kaupanger daily at 8:50, 11:30, 15:30, and 17:40 (2-hr trip). Kaupanger is a ferry landing set on the scenic Sognefjord, and little more. The little stave-type church at the edge of Kaupanger is worth a free peek. (In 1995, the Anhiller ferry dock is expected to replace the Kaupanger dock.)

▲▲**Kaupanger/Revsnes/Hornadalen/Aurland Scenic Drive**—This drive takes you over an incredible mountain pass, offers classic fjord aerial views, and winds into the pleasant fjord-side town of Aurland. Catch the Kaupanger-Revsnes ferry (13 min; at least hourly departures including 14:50, 15:30, 16:00, 17:00, 17:50, and 19:00; 40 kr for car and driver, 16 kr per passenger; tel. 57 67 81 16, reservations not allowed, arrive 20 min early on summer weekends). Note: sometime in 1995 the new Anhiller ferry dock will replace the Kaupanger dock. Leave E-68 at Erdal to make the wildly scenic and treacherous 90-minute drive to Aurland over 4,000-foot-high Hornadalen. This summer-only road passes remote mountain huts and terrifying mountain views, before its 12-hairpin zigzag descent into the Aurlandsfjord which has the best fjord views this lifetime has to offer. Stop at the first fjord view point as you begin your descent; it's the best.

Sleeping in Gudbrandsdalen Valley

This is a very popular vacation valley for Norwegians, and you'll find loads of reasonable small hotels and campgrounds with huts (*hytter* means bungalow, *rom* is private room, and *ledig* means not full) for those who aren't quite campers. These huts normally cost around 200 kr and can take from four to six people. Although they are simple, you'll have a kitchenette and access to a good WC and shower. When available, sheets rent for an extra 40 kr per person. Local TIs can find you rooms. Only in the middle three weeks of July will finding a bed without a reservation prove difficult.

Sleep code: **S**=Single, **D**=Double/Twin, **T**=Triple, **Q**=Quad, **B**=Bath/Shower, **WC**=Toilet, **CC**=Credit Card (Visa, Mastercard, Amex).

In the town of Kvam, the **Kirketeigen Ungdomssenter** (literally "Church Youth Center"), run by friendly Katrina and Hakon Olsen, welcomes travelers all year long. They have camping places (65 kr per tent or van), huts (210 kr per

4-person hut), and very simple 4-bed rooms (250 kr for 2-4 people with sheets). Sheets and blankets (60 kr) can be rented (2650 Kvam i. Gudbrandsdalen, located behind the town church, tel. 61 29 40 82, call in advance). One hundred meters away is the **Sinclair Vertshuset Motel**, 100 meters away, has an inexpensive pizzeria (DBWC-530 kr without breakfast or personality, cheaper off-season, tel. 61 29 40 24). The motel was named after a Scotsman who led a band of adventurers into this valley attempting to set up their own Scottish kingdom. They failed. (All were kilt).

Sleeping in Jotunheim
(7 kr = about $1)
Roisheim and Elvesaeter are just hotel road stops in the wild. Boverdal, a couple miles up the road, is a tiny village with a youth hostel.

Roisheim, in a marvelously remote mountain setting, is a storybook hotel comprised of a cluster of centuries-old, sod-roofed log farmhouses. Filled with antiques, Norwegian travelers, and the hard work of its harried owners, Unni and Wilfried Reinschmidt, Roisheim is a cultural end in itself. Each room is rustic, but elegant (D-700 kr, DBWC 700 kr-1,100 kr without breakfast, CC:V). Some rooms are in old log huts with low ceilings and heavy beams. The honeymooner's special has a canopy bed. Wilfried, a well-known chef, serves memorable meals. Gilded lily breakfasts are 110 kr, and a full three-course traditional dinner (one that Norway's royalty travels far to eat) is served at 19:00 (300 kr). Call ahead so they'll beprepared. (Open May to mid-October, 6 miles south of Lom on the Sognefjell Road #55 in Boverdalen, tel. 61 21 20 31, fax 61 21 21 51.)

The **Elvesaeter Hotel** is as Old World romantic as Roisheim, but cheaper and less impressed with itself (DBWC-500 kr with breakfast, CC:VMA, wonderful 130 kr buffet dinners, open June-September, a few minutes farther up road 55, just past Boverdal, tel. 61 21 20 00, fax 61 21 21 01). They also offer apartments with kitchens and all bedding (4-6 people, 500 kr-900 kr without breakfast). The Elvesaeter family has done a great job retaining the historic character of their medieval farm, even though the place is big enough to handle large tour groups. They have the dubious distinction of being, as far as I know, the only hotel in Europe that charges for its advertising flier (4 kr). It's scenic—but not that scenic.

Boverdalen Youth Hostel, just a couple of miles from Roisheim, is in another galaxy price-wise (4- to 6-bed rooms, 70 kr per bed, D-190 kr, the usual extra for sheets and non-members, hot and self-serve meals, open mid-May to September, tel. 61 21 20 64). It's in the center of a little community (store, post office, campground, and toll road up to Galdhopiggen area). The hostel is a comfortable budget value, and you'll eat with real hikers rather than car tourists.

Sleeping in Sogndal

For budget rooms in town, try the home of **Bjarne and Ella Skieldestad** (150 kr per person, kitchenette, on the town's main drag at Gravensteinsgate 10, tel. 57 67 21 83), the **Loftenes pensjonat** (DBWC-600 kr with breakfast, near the water, tel. 57 67 15 77), or the excellent **youth hostel** (beds in 1- to 4-bed rooms for 85 kr, sheets and guest membership extra, D-200 kr, hot meals and members' kitchen, at the fork in the road as you enter town, tel. 57 67 20 33, closed 10:30-16:30 and mid-August to mid-June).

Sleeping in Solvorn

The **Walaker Hotel**, a former inn and coach station, has been run by the Walaker family for 300 years (that's a lot of pressure on the next generation). In the main house, tradition drips like butter through the halls and living rooms. The rooms are simple but good, a warm family feeling pervades, and there are only patriotic hymns on the piano. The modern annex is basic and functional. The Walaker, set right on the Lustrafjord (in the perfect garden to get over a mental breakdown), is open May-September. Oda and Hermod Walaker are a wealth of information and help serve fine food (D-660 kr, DBWC-780 kr-880 kr with breakfast, dinners are worth the 220 kr splurge, CC:V, tel. 57 68 42 07, fax 57 68 45 44).

Route Tips for Drivers

Oslo Across Norway to Jotunheim: It's 2½ hours from Oslo to Lillehammer and 4 hours after that to Lom. Wind out of Oslo following signs for E-6 (not to Dramman, but for a few yards to Stockholm and then to Trondheim). In a few minutes, you're in the wide-open pastoral countryside of eastern Norway. Norway's Constitution Hall is a 5-minute detour off E-6, a couple of miles south of Eidsvoll in Eidsvoll Verk (follow the signs to Eidsvoll Bygningen).

Then, E-6 takes you along Norway's largest lake (Mjosa) through the town of Hamar, over a toll bridge (15 kr), and past more nice lake scenery into Lillehammer (site of the 1994 Winter Olympics). The old E-6 stays on the east side of the lake, is only marginally slower, and avoids the toll bridge. Signs direct you uphill from downtown Lillehammer to the Maihaugen museum. There's free parking near the pay lot (10 kr) above the entrance. Then, E-6 enters the valley of Gudbrandsdalen. From Lillehammer, cross the bridge again and follow signs to E-6/Dombas and Trondheim. At Otta, exit for Lom.

Mountain driving tips: Use low gears and lots of patience both up (to keep it cool) and down (to save your brakes). Uphill traffic gets the right-of-way, but drivers, up or down, considerately dive for the nearest fat part whenever they meet. Ask back-seat drivers not to scream until you've actually been hit or left the road.

Driving along Lustrafjord: From the little town of Nes on the west bank of the Lustrafjord, look across the fjord at the impressive Feigumfoss Waterfall. Drops and dribbles come from miles around for this 200-yard tumble. Dale, a village on the west bank, boasts a 13th-century stone Gothic church with 14th-century frescoes. It's unique and worth a peek. Skjolden, a village at the north tip of Lustrafjord, has a helpful tourist office (tel. 57 68 67 50) with advice on fjord ferries, glacier hikes, etc., and a cozy youth hostel on the river (70 kr per bed, D-160 kr, tel. 57 68 66 15).

Ferry travel: Car ferries and express boats connect towns along the Sognefjord and Bergen. Ferries go where you need them and cost roughly $4 per hour for walk-ons and $14 per hour for a car, driver, and passenger. Reservations are generally not necessary (and sometimes not possible), but in summer, especially on Friday and Sunday, I'd get one to be safe (free and easy, tel. 57 67 81 16).

From Gudvangen to Bergen (85 miles): From Gudvangen, drive up the Naeroydalen (Narrow Valley) past a river bubbling excitedly about the plunge it just took. You'll see the two giant falls just before the road marked Stalheimskleiva. Follow the sign to the little Stalheimskleiva road. This incredible road doggedly worms its way up into the ozone. My car overheated in a few minutes. Take it, but take it easy. (The main road gets you there easier—through a tunnel and 1.3-km back up a smaller road.) As you wind up, you can view the falls from several turnouts. At the top, stop for a break at the friendly but very, very touristy Stalheim Hotel. This huge eagle's-nest hotel is a stop for just about every tour group that ever saw a fjord. Here, genuine trolls sew the pewter buttons on the sweaters, and the priceless view is free.

The road continues into a mellower beauty past lakes and farms toward Voss. Tvindefossen, a waterfall with a handy campground/WC/kiosk picnic area right under it, is worth a stop. Unless you judge waterfalls by megatonnage, this 150-yard-long fall has nuclear charms. The grassy meadow and flat rocks at its base were made especially for your picnic lunch.

The highway takes you through Voss and right into Bergen. On Monday-Friday, 6:00-22:00, drivers pay a 5 kr toll as they enter Bergen. (If you're visiting Edvard Grieg's home and the nearby Fantoft stave church, now is the ideal time since you'll be driving right by them. Both are over-rated but kind of obligatory, a headache from downtown, and open until 17:30.)

BERGEN

Bergen has a rugged charm, permanently salted with robust cobbles and a rich sea-trading heritage. Norway's capital in the 12th and 13th centuries, Bergen's wealth and importance were due to its membership in the heavyweight medieval trading club of merchant cities called the Hanseatic League. Bergen still wears her rich Hanseatic heritage proudly.

Enjoy her salty market, stroll the easy-on-foot old quarter, and treat yourself to a grand Norwegian-style smorgasbord dinner. From downtown Bergen, a funicular zips you up a little mountain for a bird's eye view of this sailors' town.

Planning Your Time

Bergen can be enjoyed even on the tail end of a day's scenic train ride from Oslo before returning on the overnight train. But that teasing taste will make you wish you had more time. On a 3-week tour of Scandinavia, Bergen is worth a whole day. Start the day at the harbor-front fish market and spend the rest of the morning in the Bryggens quarter (the tour is a must).

Bergen, a geographic dead end for most, is an efficient place to end your Scandinavian tour. Consider flying home from here. (Ask your travel agent about the economic feasibility of this "open jaws" option.)

Orientation

Bergen is a romantic place with a colorful harborside fish market, old atmospheric "Hanseatic" quarter, and great people-watching. Famous for its lousy weather, Bergen gets an average of 80 inches of rain annually (compared to 30 inches in Oslo). A good year has 60 days of sunshine. With 210,000 people, it has its big city tension, parking problems, and high prices. But visitors stick mainly to the old center—easily handled on foot.

Tourist Information

On the harborfront in the old town, this TI covers Bergen and West Norway. They change money at 4 percent less than the banks (but with no 15 kr per check fee for traveler's checks, so they're okay for small exchanges or people who are stuck with small checks in Norway). They also have information and tickets for tours and concerts and a daily events board (a 5-minute walk from the train station, tel. 55 32 14 80, open May-September 8:30-21:00, Sunday 10:00-19:00; off-season 9:00-16:00, closed Sunday). The free *Bergen Guide* lists all sights, hours, and special events and has a fine map. The Bergen Card gives you 24 hours of city buses and sights admissions for 100 kr. (Train info tel. 55 96 60 50; SAS info tel. 55 99 76 10.)

Getting Around

Buses cost 12 kr per ride or 60 kr for a 48-hour Tourist Ticket (buy as you board). The best buses for a city joy ride are #1 and #4. A little red ferry chugs across the harbor every half hour for 8 kr. This poorman's cruise has great harbor views.

Sights—Bergen's Hanseatic Quarter

▲▲▲**Hanseatic Quarter**—Called the German wharf until 1940 (now just called the wharf, or Bryggen), this is Bergen's old German trading center. From 1370 to 1754, German merchants controlled Bergen's trade. In 1550, it was a German city of 2,000 workaholic merchants—walled and surrounded by 8,000 Norwegians. Bryggen, which has burned down several times, is now gentrified and boutiquish, but still lots of fun. Explore. You'll find plenty of shops, restaurants, planky alleys, leaning old wooden warehouses, good browsing, atmospheric eating, and two worthwhile museums. The following Hanseatic sights are within a 2-minute walk of each other.

▲▲▲**Walking Tour**—Every day at 11:00 and 13:00 June-August, a local historian takes visitors on an excellent 90-minute walk through the old Hanseatic town. This is a great way to get an understanding of Bergen's 900 years of history. Tours cost 50 kr and leave from the Bryggens Museum (next to the SAS hotel). This fee includes entry tickets and tours of the Hanseatic and Bryggens museums and the medieval assembly rooms called the Schotstuene (very worthwhile, but only with a guide, tel. 55 31 67 10).

▲▲▲**The Hanseatic Museum**—This wonderful little museum is in an atmospheric old merchant house furnished

Bergen and Harbor

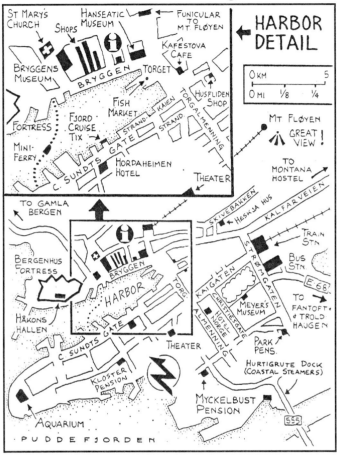

with dried fish, old ropes, an old ox-tail (used for wringing spilled cod liver oil back into the bucket), sagging steps, and cupboard beds from the early 1700s (one with a medieval pin-up). (Open daily 9:00-17:00; May and September 11:00-14:00, 30 kr included on Bryggen tour, tel. 55 31 41 89.) Drop in and ask when the next sporadic, but very good, English tour is scheduled.

▲▲▲**Bryggens Museum**—This new modern museum on the archaeological site of the earliest Bergen (1050-1500), with interesting temporary exhibits upstairs, offers almost no English information (if you take the tour, the 20 kr English guidebook is unnecessary). You can see the actual excavation for free from the window just below St. Mary's Church (15 kr, 10:00-17:00, less off-season, tel. 55 31 67 10). There is a good inexpensive cafeteria with soup and bread specials.

St. Mary's Church—Dating from about 1150, this is Bergen's oldest building and one of Norway's finest churches (10 kr, Monday-Friday in summer 11:00-16:00).

Fish Market—This famous, bustling market offers lots of smelly photo fun (Monday-Saturday 8:00-15:00). Don't miss it.

More Sights—Bergen

▲**Hakon's Hall/Rosenkrantz Tower**—These reminders of Bergen's medieval importance sit barren and boldly out of place on the harbor just beyond Bryggen. Hakon's Hall was a royal residence 700 years ago, when Bergen was the political center of Norway. Tours of both start in Hakon's Hall and leave on the hour (20 kr, 45 min, 10:00-16:00, last tour at 15:00 daily, tel. 55 31 60 67). There's a great harbor view from the tower's rooftop.

▲▲**Floibanen**—Just 2 blocks from the fish market is the steep funicular ride to the top of "Mount" Floien (1,000 feet up) for the best view of the town, surrounding islands, and fjords all the way to the west coast. There are endless hikes on top and a pleasant walk back down into Bergen. It's a popular picnic or pizza-to-go perch (28 kr round-trip, departures each way on the half-hour and often on the quarter-hour). Peppe's Pizza is a block away from the base of the lift.

▲▲**Wandering**—Bergen is a great strolling town. The harborfront is a fine place to kick back and watch the pigeons mate. Other good areas to explore are Klostergate, Knosesmanet, Ytre Markevei, and the area behind Bryggen. The modern town also has a pleasant ambience.

▲▲**Aquarium**—Small but great fun if you like fish, this aquarium, wonderfully laid out and explained in English, claims to be the second-most-visited sight in Norway. A pleasant 10-minute walk from the center, it has a cheery cafeteria with fresh fish sandwiches. (35 kr, daily 9:00-20:00, off-season 10:00-18:00, feeding times 11:00, 13:00, and 15:00, tel. 55 23 85 53, bus #4.)

▲**Old Bergen**—Gamle Bergen is a Disney-cute gathering of forty 18th- and 19th-century shops and houses offering a cutesy, cobbled look at "the old life." The town is free, and half the buildings are art galleries and gift shops. English tours departing on the hour (20 kr) get you into the twenty-or-so museum buildings. (25 kr, open daily mid-May to August 11:00-18:00, with English guided tours on the hour, tel. 55 25 78 50.) Take bus #1 or #9, from Bryggen (direction Lonborg) to Gamle Bergen (first stop after the second tunnel).

▲**Various City Tours**—The tourist information center sells tickets to several tours, including a daily 90-minute introduction at 17:00 (60 kr) and a daily 2-hour tour at 14:30 (90 kr). These tours, which leave from the TI, are barely worthwhile for a quick orientation. More fun and very informative, if you're into city tours, are the harbor tours (14:30, aboard the White Lady, tel. 55 31 43 20, from the fish market) and the tacky tourist train with English headphone tours. Both cost 60 kr for 50 minutes and leave on the hour from the harborfront.

▲**Fantoft Stave Church**—The huge preserved-in-tar, most-touristy stave church in Norway burned down in 1992. It's being rebuilt, and hopes to reopen in 1995, but it can never be the same. Situated in a quiet forest next to a mysterious stone cross, this 12th-century wooden church is bigger, but no better, than others covered in this book. It's worth a look if you're in the neighborhood, even after hours, for its evocative setting.

▲**Grieg's Home, Troldhaugen**—Norway's greatest composer spent his last years here (1885-1907), soaking up inspirational fjord beauty and composing many of his greatest works. In a very romantic Victorian setting, the ambience of the place is pleasant, even for non-fans, and essential to anyone who knows and loves Grieg's music. The house is full of memories, and his little studio hut near the water makes you want to sit down and modulate. Unfortunately, it gets the "Worst Presentation in Scandinavia for a Historical Sight Award," since it's mobbed with tour groups, offers nothing in English, and uses no imagination in mixing Grieg's music with the house. (30 kr, daily, May-September 9:30-17:30, tel. 55 91 17 91.) Ask the tourist office about concerts in the concert hall at the site (70 kr, plus 35 kr for the shuttle bus from downtown, Wednesday and Sunday at 19:30, Saturday at 14:00 in late July and August, tel. 55 97 64 99).

The TI's free *Bergen Guide* pamphlet gives bus directions to Troldhaugen. The daily bus tour (10:30, 150 kr) is worthwhile for the very informative guide and the easy transportation. If you've seen other stave churches and can't whistle anything by Grieg, skip them.

Shopping—The Husfliden Shop (just off the market at 3 Vagsalmenning) is a fine place for handmade Norwegian sweaters and goodies (good variety and quality, but expensive). Like most shops, it's open 9:00-16:30 Monday-Friday, Thursday until 19:00, Saturday 9:00-14:00. Major shops are closed on Sunday, but shop-till-you-drop tourists manage to find plenty of action even on the day of rest.

Folk Evenings—The "Fana Folklore" show is Bergen's most advertised folk evening. An old farm hosts this very touristy collection of cultural clichés, with food, music, dancing, and colorful costumes. While many think it's too gimmicky, and many think it's lots of fun, *nobody* likes the dinner. 190 kr includes the short bus trip and the meager meal. (Most nights June-August 19:00-22:30, tel. 55 91 52 40.)

The **Bergen Folklore show** is a smaller, less gimmicky program, featuring a good music-and-dance look at rural and traditional Norway. Performances are downtown at the Bryggens Museum (every Tuesday and Thursday evening mid-June to August, tickets for the 1-hour show are 70 kr at the TI or at the door, tel. 55 31 95 50).

Scenic Boats and Trains from Bergen—The TI has several brochures on tours of the nearby Hardanger and Sogne fjords. There are plenty of choices. For all the specifics on "Norway in a Nutshell," a scenic combination of buses, ferries, and trains, which can be done in a day from Bergen (7:30-14:30 or 9:00-20:00), see the chapter on Fjords, Mountains, and Valleys.

Sleeping in Bergen
(7 kr = about $1)

July through mid-August is peak season for rainy Bergen, but you should find a room just about any time without a reservation. The hotel scene is bleak (minimum 400 kr doubles) with none of the great summer discounts found in other big Nordic cities. But if you can handle showers down the hall and cook breakfast yourself in the communal kitchens, several pensions offer better rooms with a homey atmosphere and a fine central location for half the hotel prices.

The private homes I list are cheap, central, and quite professional. The cheapest dorm/hostel-style beds are not much less than the private homes, and unless the shoestring you're traveling on is really frazzled or you like to hang out with other vagabonds and hostelers, I'd stick with the private rooms. The tourist office is helpful in finding the least expensive rooms, but if you call the hotel direct, you'll save yourself the TI fee (15 kr-20 kr).

Sleep code: **S**=Single, **D**=Double/Twin, **T**=Triple, **Q**=Quad, **B**=Bath/Shower, **WC**=Toilet, **CC**=Credit Card (**V**isa, **M**astercard, **A**mex).

Sleeping in Hotels and Pensions

If you must have a uniformed person behind the key desk, the prestigious old **Hotel Hordaheimen** is central, just off the harbor, and your best budget hotel bet. Run by the same alcohol-free, give-the-working-man-a-break organization that brought you Kaffistova restaurants, their cafeteria, open late, serves traditional, basic (drab), inexpensive meals (DBWC-970 kr, or 790 kr in summer with reservations no more than 48 hours in advance, CC:VMA, 18 C. Sundts Gate, tel. 55 23 23 20, fax 55 23 49 50).

Mycklebust Pension is a family-run explosion of homeyness, offering better rooms than the Hordaheimen, but pension rather than hotel services. It's friendly, central (a 5-minute walk to market), with your own kitchen and laundry service, and showers down the hall (D-400 kr, DBWC-450 kr or a family-of-four room, no breakfast, 19 Rosenberggate, tel. 55 90 16 70.)

Kloster Pension, in a funky cobbled neighborhood 4 blocks off the harbor, has basic 380 kr-550 kr doubles including breakfast (D-380 kr, DBWC-550 kr, 12 Klosteret, tel. 55 90 21 58, fax 55 23 30 22). **Fagerheim Pension**, offers some of the cheapest doubles in town (D-320 kr, breakfast extra; 49A Kalvedals veien, up King Oscar's Gate half a mile, tel. 55 31 01 72). **Park Pension** is classy, nearly a hotel, and in a wonderful neighborhood—central but residential. People who have the money for a cheap hotel, but want Old World lived-in elegance, love this place (D-600 kr, DBWC-700 kr with breakfast, CC:VMA, 35 Harold Harfagres Gate, tel. 55 32 09 60, fax 55 31 03 34).

Sleeping in Rooms in Private Homes

Since the Bergen hotel owners don't quite understand the magic of the marketplace, there are more private homes opening up than ever. While (for a price) the TI would love to help you out, here are several you can book direct.

Alf and Elisabeth Heskja are a young couple with four doubles, one shared shower/WC, and a kitchen. Located 5 minutes from the train station (down Kong Oscars Gate, uphill on D Krohns Gate, up the stairs at the end of the block) on Skivebakken, the steep cobbled "most painted street in Bergen." This is my home in Bergen, and far better than the hostel for budget train travelers. (D-250 kr, 17 Skivebakken, 5018 Bergen, tel. 55 31 30 30, call in advance). They also have a house at Lille Ovregatan 20-C, a quiet road leading to the funicular, with similar rooms for the same price. Also on Skivebakken is the **Olsnes home** (S-155 kr, D-260 kr, DBWC-310 kr, 24 Skivebakken, tel. 55 31 20 44). These are both central and very cheap, quite private, and lacking a lot of chatty interaction with your hosts.

Mrs. Keri Michelsen rents rooms from her home in the town center (D-260 kr, near the Park Pension at Harold Harfagres gate 3, tel. 55 32 56 31). **The Sortland family** is also right downtown (S-140 kr, D-280 kr, no breakfast, near Hotel Norge at Vestre Torvgate 20-B, 5015 Bergen, tel. 55 31 88 67).

The Vagenes family has six doubles in a large comfortable house on the edge of town (D-220 kr, no breakfast, J.L. Mowinckelsvei 95, tel. 55 16 11 01). Not so central, but 10 minutes from downtown on bus #60. From downtown cross the Puddefjordsbroen bridge (road 555), go through the upper tunnel on road 540, and turn left on J.L. Mowinckelsvei until you reach Helgeplasset Street, just past the Hogesenter. **Edel Olfarnes** rents out three double rooms (summer only) overlooking Bergen two stops up the Floibanen lift (D-270 kr, Fjellveisen 78, 5019 Bergen, tel. 55 31 72 78).

Sleeping in Hostels

Intermission offers 40 cheap mattresses in three coed dorms for 95 kr (open mid-June to mid-August, 8:00-11:00, 17:00-24:00 only, kitchen, free laundry machines, Kalfarsveien 8, a 5-minute walk from the train station, tel. 55 31 32 75).

YMCA Interrail Center—For 90 kr you get a mattress on the floor in 10- to 30-person rooms (one for girls, the others mixed). You must have a sleeping bag. (Open 7:00-11:00, 17:00-24:00, mid-June to early September, 5 minutes from the station, near the center in a pink house at Korskirke alm #4, tel. 55 31 72 52.)

Montana Youth Hostel (IYHF)—One of Europe's best hostels, its drawbacks are the remote location and relatively high price. Still, the bus connections (#4, 15 minutes from the center) and the facilities (modern 5-bed rooms, classy living room, no curfew, huge parking lot, member's kitchen) are excellent. (145 kr per bed with a big breakfast, sheets 36 kr, non-members pay 25 kr extra, 30 Johan Blydts Vei, tel. 55 29 29 00.)

Eating in Bergen

The **Kaffistova Cafeteria**, facing the fish market, is a good basic food value. Fine atmosphere (ground floor, better than fast food; first floor, self-service cafeteria; second floor, café serving meals). Ground floor is open until 22:00 (good hot pancake meat rolls); café only until 19:00, closed earlier off-season. For similar old Norwegian fare, eat at the borderline dreary cafeteria in the **Hordaheimen Hotel**—great prices and lots of *lefse*. The **Augusta Conditori and Lunchsalon** (next to Hotel Hordaheimen at C. Sundtsgate 24) serves good meals at a reasonable price in a cheery-classy atmosphere. Open 10:00-18:00.

Bryggeloffet and Bryggestuen (one restaurant with one menu on two levels with two different styles at #6 in the Bryggen harborfront) offers good (but smoky) atmosphere, and seafood and traditional meals for around 100 kr. Small servings, but more potatoes on request. The Dagens Menu is 60 kr (off-season only). There are plenty of classy atmospheric places along the Bryggen harborfront.

The **Unicorn** offers Bergen's top seafood buffet, but is quite expensive (140 kr, Monday-Saturday 12:00-16:00). And **Kjottborsen** (literally, "meat market," 6 Vaskerelven, tel. 55 23 14 59) is a splurge local carnivores enjoy.

Hotel Norge's "Koltbord" buffet—Bergen's ritziest hotel serves a daily all-you-can-eat spread in its classy Ole Bull restaurant—hot dishes, seafood, and desserts rich in both memories and calories (155 kr, enter 12:00-16:00, tel. 55 21 01 00).

Bergen's "in" cafés are stylish, cozy, small, open very late, and a great place to experience the local yuppie scene. The trendy **Café Opera** is good (50 kr dinners, 30 kr soup and bread specials, often with live music, always with live locals, English newspapers, chess, open to the wee hours).

The **Zachariassbryggen** restaurant complex has is a good pub (Freddie's) with piano music (open late, popular with locals), located right on the Torget, or harbor square. For a louder crowd and a younger scene, try the **Maxime Bergen's Polar Bear Bar** (light lunches for 30 kr, "cheapest dinners in town," Ole Bulls Plass 9, around the corner from the taxi station and TI, serves food until about 20:00).

Transportation Connections

Bergen is only conveniently connected to **Oslo** by train (3/day, 7 scenic hrs). To get to **Stockholm** or **Copenhagen** or even **Trondheim**, you'll be going via Oslo unless you fly. Before buying any long train ticket from Bergen, look into cheap flights. You might be pleasantly surprised with what you find and you might not.

Cruising to Newcastle, England: The Color Line (tel. 55 54 86 60) sails from Bergen to **Newcastle, England** on Tuesday, Friday, and Sunday, June-August. The cheapest peak-season crossing for the 22-hour trip is 880 kr with a reclining chair (sleeperette) on Tuesday or Sunday. Cars with up to 4 passengers cost about 2,700 kr.

SOUTH NORWAY'S SETESDAL VALLEY

Welcome to the remote—and therefore very traditional—Setesdal Valley. Probably Norway's most authentic cranny, the valley is a mellow montage of sod-roofed water mills, ancient churches, derelict farmhouses, yellowed recipes, and gentle scenery. The locals practice fiddles and harmonicas, rose painting, whittling, and gold and silverwork. The famous Setesdal filigree echoes the rhythmical design of the Viking and middle ages.

The Setesdal Valley joined the 20th century with the construction of the valley highway in the 1950s. All along the valley you'll see the unique two-story storage sheds called *stabburs* (the top floor stored clothes; the bottom, food) and many sod roofs. Even the bus stops have rooftops the local goats love to munch.

In the high country, just over the Sessvatn summit (3,000 ft.), you'll see goat herds and summer farms. If you see an *Ekte Geitost* sign, that means homemade goat cheese is for sale. (It's sold cheaper and in more manageable sizes in grocery stores.) To some it looks like a decade's accumulation of ear wax. I think it's delicious. Remember, *ekte* means all-goat—real strong (the more popular and easier-to-eat regular goat cheese has cow's-milk cheese mixed in).

Each town in the Setesdal Valley has a weekly rotating series of hikes and activities for the regular, stay-put-for-a-week visitor. The upper valley is dead in the summer, but enjoys a bustling winter. This is easygoing sightseeing— nothing earthshaking. Let's just pretend you're on vacation.

Planning Your Time

Frankly, without a car, Setesdal is not worth the trouble. There are no trains, bus schedules are as sparse as the population, and the sights are best for joy-riding. If you're driving in Bergen and want to get back to Denmark, this route is more interesting than repeating Oslo. On a 3-week Scandinavian trip, I'd do it in one long day this way:

6:00–Leave Bergen.
8:00–Catch the Kvanndal ferry to Utne.

9:00–Say good-bye to the last fjord at Odda.

12:00–Lunch in Hovden at the top of Setesdal Valley.

13:00–Frolic south with a few short stops through the valley.

18:00–Arrive in Kristiansand (dinner and a movie?).

23:00–Board boat for overnight crossing.

Setesdal Valley

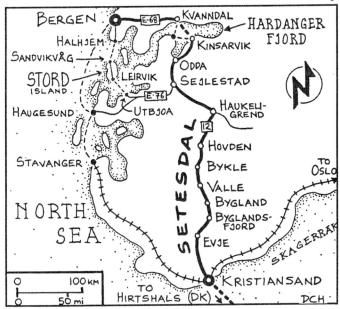

Sights—Setesdal Valley

These sights are listed from north to south.

Odda—At the end of the Hardanger fjord, just past the huge zinc and copper industrial plant, you'll hit the industrial town of Odda (well-stocked TI for whole region and beyond, tel. 53 64 12 97). Odda brags that Kaiser Wilhelm came here a lot, but he's dead and I'd drive right through. If you want to visit the tongue of a glacier, drive to Buer and hike an hour to Buerbreen. From Odda, drive into the land of boulders, where rocks so big that trees grow on them seem to be hurled into the fields by the mighty waterfalls that almost line the road. Stop at the giant double fall (on the left, pull out on the right, drive slowly through it if you need a car wash).

Roldal—Higher up, the old town of Roldal is trying to develop some tourism. Drive straight through. Its old church isn't worth the time or money to see. Lakes, like frosted mirrors, make desolate huts come in pairs. Haukeliseter, a group of sod-roofed buildings filled with cultural clichés and tour groups, offers reasonable (40 kr-50 kr) hot meals with a great lakeside setting. If you have yet to try the traditional romegrot porridge, this is a good time.

If you plan to sleep in Haukeligrend, **Haukeli Turistheim Pensjonat** offers quaint old rooms (in the quaint old half of the building), a feel-at-home Old World living room, a ping-pong table, and no breakfast but a reasonable cafeteria (D-250 kr, at the junction of roads #76 and #12 in Haukeligrend, about 6 hours out of Bergen, 30 minutes before Hovden, tel. 35 07 01 26).

Hovden—Right at the top of the Setesdal Valley, Hovden is a ski resort (2,500 feet high), barren in the summer and painfully in need of charm. Hovden is for nature lovers. Locals come here to walk and relax for a week. There are good walks offering a chance to see reindeer, moose, arctic fox, and wabbits—so they say. Every other day a chairlift takes summer visitors to its nearby 3,700-foot peak. The Hegni center, on the lake at the south edge of town, rents canoes for 30 kr an hour. A new super indoor spa/pool complex, the Hovden Badeland (80 kr, daily 10:00-19:00) provides a much-needed way to spend an otherwise dreary (and very likely) drizzly early evening here. (TI, open Monday-Friday 8:00-16:00, tel. 37 93 96 30.)

If you stay in Hovden, the **Hovdehytta Hostel**, a big old ski chalet with an inviting ski lodge atmosphere (large dining room, open fire in the living room), offers clean, modern bunk-bed doubles with a large breakfast for 320 kr (40 kr extra for sheets and those without a hostel card). Good 70 kr dinners must be ordered by 15:00 (tel. 37 93 95 22). Built in 1911, this is the oldest place in town and the only cozy and reasonable accommodations in this booming winter resort of sprawling ranch-style ski hotels.

▲**Dammar Vatnedalsvatn**—Just south of Hovden is a 2-mile side trip to a 400-foot-high rock-pile dam. Great view, impressive rockery. This is the highest dam in northern Europe. Read the chart. Sit out of the wind a few rows down the rock pile and ponder the vastness of Norwegian wood.

▲**Bykle**—The most interesting folk museum and church in Setesdal are in the teeny town of Bykle. The 17th-century interior has two balconies—one for men and one for women (5 kr, mid-June to mid-August 10:00-17:00, Saturday and Sunday 12:00-17:00).

Bykle has a wonderful little open-air folk museum. The **Huldreheimen Museum** is a typical 800-year-old seterhouse used when the cattle spent the summer high in the mountains. Follow the sign up a road to a farm high above the town, park, then hike a steep 150 yards into Norway's medieval peasant past—fine view, six houses filled with old stuff, and a good English information sheet. (10 kr, open mid-June to mid-August 10:00-18:00, Saturday and Sunday 12:00-18:00). Off-season, ask the friendly old woman who lives on the farm to let you take a look.

Grasbrokke—On the east side of the main road (at the Grasbrokke sign) you'll see an old water mill (1630). A few minutes farther south is a "Picnic and WC" sign on west. Exit onto that little road. You'll pass another old water mill with a fragile rotten log sluice. At the second picnic turnout (just before this roadlet returns to the highway, you'll find a covered picnic table for rainy lunches), turn out and frolic along the river rocks.

Flateland—One mile east, off the main road, is the Setesdal museum (Rygnestadtunet), offering more of what you saw at Bykle (two buildings, 20 kr, daily mid-June to mid-August 10:00-18:00, otherwise 11:00-17:00). Unless you're a glutton for culture, I wouldn't do both.

▲**Valle**—This is Setesdal's prettiest village (but don't tell Bykle). In the center you'll find fine silver and gold work at Grete and Ornulfs Sylvsmie, and traditional lunches in the cozy Bergtun Hotel (daily specials, 70 kr, 12:00-22:00), the *husflid* shop (offering traditional homemade crafts and old-fashioned *lefsa* cooking demonstrations), and a fine suspension bridge for little boys of any age who still like to bounce (and for anyone interested in a great view of the strange mountains over the river that look like polished petrified mud slides). European rock climbers, tired of the over-climbed Alps, often provide spectators with their sport. Is anyone climbing? (The TI is open mid-June to mid-August, Monday-Friday 10:00-17:00, Saturday 10:00-14:00, closed Sunday, less off-season, tel. 37 93 73 12.)

If you stay in Valle, try the **Bergtun Hotel**, run by Gunnar Oiestad, a real folksy, sit-a-spell Setesdal lodging. It's full of traditional furniture, paintings, and carvings in each charming room. (D-400 kr [bunks] to 500 kr [four-poster beds] with breakfast, hearty traditional lunch specials [*dagens rett*] from 70 kr are served 12:00-22:00, Valle i Setesdal, tel. 37 93 72 70.)

Nomeland—Sylvartun, the silversmith with the valley's most aggressive publicity department, demonstrates the Setesdal specialty in a traditional log cabin from the 17th century and a free little gallery/museum. He gives a free fiddle concert most days in July at 14:00.

Grendi—The Ardal Church (1827) has a runestone in its yard. And for good measure, 300 yards south of the church, is an oak tree said to be 900 years old.

Evje—A huge town by Setesdal standards (3,500 people), Evje is famous for its gems and mines. Fancy stones fill the shops here. Only rockhounds would find the nearby mines fun (for a small fee you can hunt for gems). The super-for-rockhounds new Setesdal Mineral Park is on the main road, 3 km south of town. For modern, bright, functional doubles in Evje, stay with the **Haugen family** (two-bunk rooms for 180 kr, 220 kr with sheets, a pleasant garden, a kitchenette, and a huge stuffed moose in the garage) on the Arendal Road (last house on the left, see Rom sign, tel. 37 93 08 88).

Kristiansand

This "capital of the south" has 60,000 inhabitants, a pleasant, grid-plan Renaissance layout (the Kvadraturen), a famous zoo with Norway's biggest amusement park (6 miles toward Oslo on the main road), and lots of big boats going to England and Denmark. It's the closest thing to a beach resort in Norway, and a pleasant place to stroll.

The Kvadraturen center, around the bustling pedestrian market street, is the shopping/eating/people-watching/browsing town center. Walk along the Strand Promenaden (marina) and to the Christiansholm Fortress. You'll find plenty of Kafeterias, a Peppe's Pizza (open until 23:00, salad bar, on Gyldenloves), and budget ethnic restaurants. For classy Norwegian dining (with classy Norwegians) or just a beer with a view, visit the Sjohoset (on the harbor at Ostre Strandgate 12). For the best dinner in town, splurge at Bak Garden (Tollbodgatan 15, hiding in the center). There are two cinema complexes (50 kr, 6 screens, showing movies in English, 50 kr, check schedules at TI) within 2 blocks of the Color Line docks and the TI.

The TI is at Dronningengate 2 (daily 7:00-19:30, Sunday 12:00-19:00; off-season Monday-Friday 8:00-16:00 only, tel. 38 02 60 65). The bank at the Color Line terminal opens for each arrival and departure (even the midnight ones) and is reasonable.

Sleeping in Kristiansand

Your best modern, comfy, and cozy bet is **Hotel Sjoglott.** Friendly Tore Kjostvedt gives his small hotel lots of class (S-350 kr, D-490 kr, DBWC-550 kr with breakfast, CC:VM, near the harbor on a quiet street at Ostre Strandgt 25, tel. 38 02 21 20, fax 38 02 18 82). Otherwise, Kristiansand hotels are expensive and nondescript. The cheapest one, the musty old **Bondeheimen** (D-440 kr, DBWC-640 kr with breakfast, CC:VMA, tel. 38 02 44 40), charges 550 kr for a double with breakfast and shower. The **Hotel Norge** (tel. 38 02 00 00) is more modern and expensive. The **youth hostel** (tel. 38 09 53 69) is cheap, but not so central.

Transportation Connections

Kristiansand, Norway to Hirtshals, Denmark: The Color Line ferry sails daily and nightly from Kristiansand in Norway to Hirtshals in Denmark (usually daily departures at about 8:00, 13:30, 19:00, and 00:30, mid-June to late-August; 8:30, 19:30, and 20:30 the rest of the year). The trip takes just over 4 hours (the overnight ride is slower to arrive at 6:30). Passengers pay 84 kr-338 kr (July and weekends are most expensive). A car costs 210 kr-480 kr. The "car package" lets five in a car travel for 1,020 kr (summer Monday-Thursday). There are decent smorgasbords, music, duty-free shopping, a desk to process your Norwegian duty-free tax rebates, and a decent bank for small changes (no fee).

As soon as you're ready to commit yourself to a firm date, call Color Line to make a reservation. Their standard ticketing process is to accept telephone reservations to be paid when you get to the dock. Color Line's information and reservation line is open daily 7:00-23:00, tel. 38 07 88 88, in Kristiansand. Or you can use their office in Oslo (tel. 22 94 44 70), Bergen (tel. 55 54 86 60), or New York (c/o Bergen Line, tel. 212/986-2711, fax 212/983-1275). Ask about specials. Round-trip fares can be lower than one-way fares.

If you take the night boat, you'll save the cost of a hotel. Enjoy an evening in Kristiansand, board the night boat, and sleep (or vomit) as you sail to Denmark. Beds on board are reasonable (reclining seats euphemistically called "sleeperettes" are 35 kr; simple curtains-for-privacy couchettes are 55 kr; a bed in a 4-berth room is around 100 kr; and a bed in a private double with shower ranges from 125 kr-380 kr per person). You owe yourself this comfort if you're doing something as efficient as spending this night traveling. I slept so well, I missed the Denmark landing and ended up crossing three times! After chewing me out, the captain said it happens a lot. Set your alarm or spend an extra day at sea.

Route Tips for Drivers

Bergen to Kristiansand (10 hours): Your first key connection is the Kvanndal-Utne ferry (a 2-hr drive from Bergen, departures at 6:45, 7:35, 8:25, and 9:00, tel. 55 23 87 80 to confirm times, reservations not possible, breakfast in cafeteria in boat's basement?). If you make the 8:00, your day will be more relaxed. Driving comfortably, with no mistakes or traffic, it's 2 hours from your Bergen hotel to the ferry dock. Leaving Bergen is a bit confusing. Pretend you're going to Oslo on the road to Voss (signs for Nestune, Landas, Nattland, 585, E16). About a half hour out of town, leave the Voss road after a long tunnel on road #7 for Norheimsund. This road, as treacherous for the famed beauty of the Hardanger Fjord it hugs as for its skinniness, is faster and safer if you beat the traffic (which you will with this plan).

The ferry drops you in Utne, where a lovely thread of a road will take you to Otta and on up into the scenic mountains. From Haukeligrend, turn south and wind up to

Sessvatn at 3,000 feet. You're entering Setesdal Valley. It's all downhill from here, following the Otra River for 140 miles south to the major port town of Kristiansand. The road is good and scenic. The traffic is sparse. Skip the few smaller secondary routes. As you enter Kristiansand, simply follow the signs for Denmark.

STOCKHOLM

If I had to call one European city home, it would be Stockholm. Surrounded by water and woods, bubbling with energy and history, Sweden's stunning capital is green, clean, and underrated.

Crawl through Europe's best-preserved old warship and relax on a canal boat tour. Browse the cobbles and antique shops of the lantern-lit old town and take a spin through Skansen, Europe's first and best open-air folk museum. Marvel at Stockholm's glittering city hall, modern department stores, art museums, and futuristic suburbs.

While progressive and sleek, Stockholm respects its heritage. Throughout the summer, mounted bands parade each noontime through the heart of town from Nybroplan to the royal palace, announcing the changing of the guard and turning even the most dignified tourist into a scampering kid. The Gamla Stan (Old Town) celebrates the Midsummer festivities (late June) with the down-home vigor of a rural village, forgetting that it's the core of a gleaming 20th-century metropolis. Stockholm also goes wild during its "Water Festival" (10 days in early August).

Planning Your Time

On a 2- to 3-week trip through Scandinavia, Stockholm is worth 2 days. Efficient train travelers sleep in and out for 2 days in the city with only one night in a hotel. (Copenhagen and Oslo trains arrive at about 8:00 and depart at about 23:00.) To be even more cheap and efficient, you could use the luxury Stockholm-Helsinki as your hotel for two nights (spending a day in Helsinki) and have 2 days in Stockholm without a hotel (e.g. Copenhagen; night train Stockholm, day in Stockholm; night boat Helsinki, day in Helsinki; night boat Stockholm, day in Stockholm; night train Oslo). That may sound crazy, but it gives you 3 interesting and inexpensive days of travel fun. Spend 2 days in Stockholm this way:

Day 1: Arrive by train (or the night before by car), do station chores (reserve next ride, change money, pick up map, "This Week," and a Stockholm Card at the Hotellcentralens TI), check into hotel. At 9:30 catch 1-hour English tour on

Sweden

the Tourist Line bus; 11:00 tour Wasa warship, picnic; 13:00 tour Nordic Museum; 15:00 Skansen; catch 16:00 open-air folk museum tour; 19:00 folk dancing, possible smorgasbord and evening popular dancing. Or wander Gamla Stan in the evening.

Day 2: Do the 10:00 city hall tour, climb the city hall tower for a fine view; 12:00 catch the changing of the guard at the palace, tour royal palace or explore Gamla Stan, picnic on 1-hour city boat tour; 16:00 browse the modern city center around Kungstradgarden, Sergels Torg, Hotorget market and indoor food hall, and Drottninggatan area.

Orientation (tel. code: 08)

Greater Stockholm's 1.4 million residents live on 14 islands, which are woven together by fifty bridges. Visitors need only concern themselves with five islands: **Norrmalm** (downtown, with most hotels, shopping areas, and the train station), **Gamla Stan** (the old city of winding lantern-lit streets, antique shops, and classy glassy cafés clustered around the royal palace), **Sodermalm** (aptly called Stockholm's Brooklyn, residential and untouristy), **Skeppsholmen** (the small, very central traffic-free park island with the Modern Art Museum and two fine youth hostels), and **Djurgarden** (literally "deer garden," Stockholm's wonderful green playground, with many of the city's top sights).

Tourist Information

Hotellcentralen is primarily a room-finding service (in the central train station), but its friendly staff adequately handles all your sightseeing and transportation questions. This is the place for anyone arriving by train to arrange accommodations, buy the Tourist Card, and pick up free brochures, city map, *Stockholm This Week* (which lists opening hours and directions to all the sights and special events), and brochures on whatever else you need (city walks, parking, jazz boats, excursions, bus routes, shopping, etc.). While *This Week* has a decent map, the 14 kr map covers more area and bus

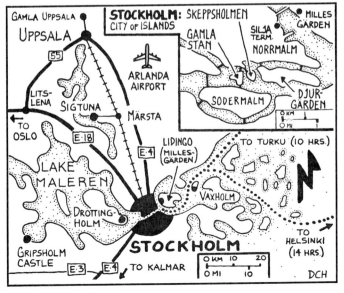

Greater Stockholm

routes. It's worth the extra money if you'll be using the buses. (Open daily June-August 7:00-21:00; May and September 8:00-19:00, shorter hours off-season; tel. 08/240880, fax 791-8666.)

Sweden House (*Sverige Huset*), Stockholm's official tourist information office (a short walk from the station on Kungstradgarden), is very good but usually more crowded than the Hotellcentralen. They've got pamphlets on everything; an "excursion shop" for transportation, day trip and bus tour information, and tickets; and an English library and reading room upstairs with racks of 1 kr information on various aspects of Swedish culture and one state's attempt at cradle-to-grave happiness. (Open June-August, 8:00-18:00, Saturday-Sunday 9:00-17:00; off-season 9:00-18:00, Saturday-Sunday 9:00-15:00; Hamngatan 27, tel. 08/789-2490 for info, 789-2415 for tickets; T-bana: Kungstradgarden.)

Getting Into and Around Stockholm

Arriving at the Train Station

Stockholm's central train station (information tel. toll free in Sweden 020/757575 for trains within Sweden, 227940 for international train info) is a wonderland of services, shops, and people going places. The Interrail Center kiosk in the center is for general help (especially for young travelers). The Hotellcentralen TI is as good as the city TI nearby. There is a Viking Line office if you're sailing to Finland. The ForEx long-hours exchange counter changes traveler's checks for only a 15 kr fee. The Tourist Line bus stops immediately in front of the station.

Parking in Stockholm

Only a Swedish meatball would drive his car in Stockholm. Park it and use the public transit. But parking is confusing, a major hassle, and expensive. Unguarded lots generally aren't safe. Take everything into your hotel, or hostel or pay for a garage. The tourist office has a "Parking in Stockholm" brochure. Those hosteling on Skeppsholmen feel privileged with their 25 kr-a-day island parking passes. Those with the Stockholm Card can park free in a big central garage or at any meter for the duration of the ticket.

Ask for your parking card and specifics when you get your Stockholm Card. There's a safe and reasonable (10 kr per day) garage at Ropsten—the last subway station (near the Silja line terminal). Those sailing to Finland can solve all parking worries by long-term parking on arrival in Stockholm at either terminal's safe and reasonable parking lot (60 kr per day).

Public Transportation

The complete hostess, Stockholm complements her many sightseeing charms with great information services, a fine bus and subway system, and special passes to take the bite out of the city's cost (or at least limit it to one vicious budgetary gash).

Buses and the subway system work on the same tickets. Ignore the zones since everything I mention (except Drottningholm and Carl Millesgarden) are in zone one. Each 13 kr ticket is valid for 1 hour (10-packs cost 85 kr). The subway, called T-bana or tunnelbana, gets you where you want to go very quickly. Ride it just for the futuristic drama of being a human mole (transit info tel. 600-1000). The *"Tourist Card"* (free run of all public transport; 24 hrs/60 kr, 72 hrs/115 kr, sold at TIs and newsstands) is not necessary if you're getting the Stockholm card (see below). The 72-hour pass includes the harbor ferry and admission to Skansen, Grona Lund, and the Kaknas Tower.

The handy **Tourist Line Bus Route** runs mid-June to mid-August, and does a figure-eight, stopping at each of Stockholm's 15 major sights (Swedish-language departures every 15 minutes, English-language tours hourly, schedule in Stockholm Card booklet). You can get off and on as you please to "do the circuit" at your leisure. It's free with the Stockholm Card (40 kr without). Do the entire 50-minute circuit in English for a cheap, easy overview.

It seems too good to be true, but each year I pinch myself and the **Stockholm Card** is still there. This 24-hour 175 kr pass (sold at TIs and ship terminals) gives you free run of all public transit, free use of the Tourist Line Bus, free entry to virtually every sight (71 places), free 1-hour city boat tours, free parking, a handy sightseeing handbook, and the substantial pleasure of doing everything without considering the cost (many of Stockholm's sights are worth the time but not the steep individual ticket costs). This pays for itself if you do Skansen, the Wasa, and the short boat tour. If you enter Skansen on your 24th hour (and head right for the 30 kr aquarium) you get a few extra hours. (Parents get an added bonus: two children under 18, go along for free with each adult pass.)

Harbor Shuttle Ferries

Throughout the summer, ferries connect Stockholm's two most interesting sightseeing districts. They sail from Nybroplan and Slussen to Djurgarden, landing next to the Vasa and Skansen (15 kr, every 20 min).

Stockholm Center

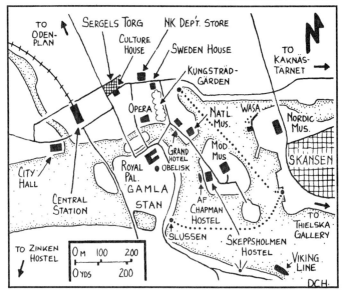

Sights—Downtown Stockholm

▲Kungstradgarden—The King's Garden square is the downtown people-watching center. Watch the life-sized game of chess and enjoy the free concerts at the bandstand. Surrounded by the Sweden House, the NK department store, the harborfront, and tour boats, it's the place to feel Stockholm's pulse (with discretion).

▲▲**Sergels Torg**—The heart of modern Stockholm, between Kungstradgarden and the station, is worth a wander. Enjoy the colorful and bustling underground mall and dip into the Gallerien mall. Visit the Kulturhuset, a center for reading, relaxing, and socializing designed for normal people (but welcoming tourists) with music, exhibits, hands-on fun, and an insight into contemporary Sweden. (Free, daily 11:00-17:00, often later, tel. 700-0100.) From Sergels Torg walk up the pedestrian mall, Drottninggatan to Hotorget (see Eating).

▲▲**City Hall**—The Stadshuset is an impressive mix of 8 million bricks, 19 million chips of gilt mosaic, and lots of Stockholm pride. One of Europe's most impressive modern (1923) buildings and site of the Nobel Prize banquet, it's particularly enjoyable and worthwhile for its entertaining tours (30 kr, daily June-August at 10:00, 11:00, 12:00, and 14:00; off season at 10:00 and 12:00, tel. 785-9074, just behind the station, bus #48 or #62). Climb the 350-foot tower for the best possible city view (10:00-16:30, May-September only, 10 kr or free with City Hall ticket). The City Hall also has a TI and a good cafeteria with 55 kr lunches.

▲**Orientation Views**—Try to get a bird's-eye perspective on this wonderful urban mix of water, parks, concrete, and people from the City Hall tower (see above), the Kaknäs Tower (at 500 feet, the tallest building in Scandinavia, 20 kr, May-August 9:00-22:00, tel. 667-8030, bus #69 from Nybroplan or Sergels Torg), the observatory in Skansen, or the top of the Katarina elevator (5 kr, near Slussen subway stop, then walk behind Katarinavagen through classy homes and grand views).

▲**Mini-Orientation Bus Tour**—For a quick big-bus orientation tour, consider those that leave from the Royal Opera House (75 kr, 50 min, 10:00, 11:00, 12:00, 14:00, 15:00, mid-June to late-August, tel. 411 70 23). They also organize 75-minute old town walks (75 kr). For a free self-guided tour, follow the walk laid out in the Stockholm *This Week* publication.

▲**City Boat Tour**—For a good floating look at Stockholm, and a pleasant break, consider a sightseeing cruise. Tour boats leave regularly from in front of the Grand Hotel (tel. 23 33 75). The Historical Stockholm tour (70 kr, 1 hr, departing on the hour 10:00-16:00, late June to mid-August) offers the best informative introduction. The "Under the Bridges" tour (120 kr, 2 hrs, May-September) is basically the first tour with an hour of extra territory. The "Royal Canal" tour (70 kr, 1 hr, mid-May to mid-September) is a scenic joyride through lots of greenery. Their 1-hour tours are free with the Stockholm Card.

▲**National Museum**—It's mediocre by European standards, but small, central, uncrowded, and very user-friendly. The highlights are several Rembrandts, Rubens, a fine group of impressionists, works by the popular and good-to-get-to-know local artists Carl Larsson and Anders Zorn, and some Russian icons. (40 kr, free on Friday, open 11:00-17:00, Tuesday 11:00-20:00, closed Monday; August some Tuesdays until 18:00 because of special concerts, tel. 666-4250).

Museum of Modern Art—This bright and cheery gallery is as far out as can be, with Picasso, Braque, and lots of goofy dada art (such as the *Urinal* and the *Goat with Tire*). It's in a pleasant park on Skeppsholmen. (30 kr, free Thursday, open Tuesday-Friday 11:00-21:00, Saturday-Sunday 11:00-17:00, closed Monday).

Sights—Stockholm's Gamla Stan (Old Town)

▲▲**Gamla Stan**—Stockholm's old island core is charming, fit for a film, and full of antique shops, street lanterns, painted ceilings, and surprises. Spend some time here, browse, enjoy a café, or get to know a shopkeeper. At the tip of the island is Slussen (Swedish for "locks"), where the salty Baltic meets the 1½-foot-higher Lake Malaren (with water so fresh that local politicians brush their teeth with it).

Military Parade—Starting at the Army Museum (daily at 12:00, Sunday at 13:00), the parade culminates at the Royal Palace for the changing of the guard.

▲▲**Royal Palace**—The stately exterior encloses 608 rooms (locals brag that that's one more than Britain's Buckingham Palace) of glittering baroque and rococo decor. There are eight different sights with separate admissions here. Most important are the apartments (30 kr, Tuesday-Saturday 10:00-15:00, Sunday and Monday 12:00-15:00; May-August 12:00-15:00, closed Monday the rest of the year). The Royal

Treasury is another ticket (25 kr, similar hours, no samples, tel. 789-8500).

Riksdag—You can tour Sweden's parliament buildings if you'd like a firsthand look at its government. (Free hourly tours in English throughout the summer, usually Monday-Friday at 12:30 and 14:00; off-season at 13:30, but call 786-4000 to confirm).

Museum of Medieval Stockholm (30 kr, July-August 11:00-16:00, Tuesday, Wednesday, Thursday until 18:00; September-June 11:00-16:00, closed Monday; the 5 kr English guide flier is not necessary since the exhibits are well-described in English, enter from the park in front of the Parliament), while grade-schoolish, gives you the best look at medieval Stockholm. The Stromparterren park, with its Carl Milles statue of the "Sun Singer" greeting the day is a pleasant place for a sightseeing break (but an expensive place for a potty break—use the free WC in the museum).

Riddarholm Church—This final resting place for about 600 years of Sweden's royalty is pretty lifeless (10 kr, May-August 10:00-15:00, Sunday 12:00-15:00, less in September, tel. 789-8500).

Sights—Stockholm's Djurgarden

▲▲▲**Skansen**—Europe's original and best open-air folk museum, Skansen is a huge park gathering over 150 historic buildings (homes, churches, schoolhouses, etc.) transplanted from all corners of Sweden. Tourists can explore this Swedish culture on a lazy Susan, seeing folk crafts in action and wonderfully furnished old interiors. In the town quarter (top of the escalator), potters, glassblowers (especially important if you'll be missing Sweden's glass country to the south), and other craftspeople are busy doing their traditional thing in a re-created Old World Stockholm.

Spreading out from there, the sprawling park is designed to show northern Swedish culture and architecture in its north (top of the park map) and southern Sweden in the south. Excellent, free 1-hour guided walks (from Bollnastorget info stand at top of escalator) paint a fine picture of old Swedish lifestyles (usually daily at 13:00 and 16:00 June-August). There's folk dancing daily in summer at 19:00, Sunday at 14:30 and 16:00, and public dancing to live bands nightly (20:30-23:30, call for evening theme—jazz, folk, rock, or disco). The Aquarium (50 kr, 10:00-20:00) is the only admission not covered on your entry ticket.

Kids love Skansen, especially its zoo (ride a life-size wooden Dala-horse and stare down a hedgehog) and Lill' Skansen (Punch 'n' Judy, mini-train, and pony ride fun daily from 10:30 till at least 16:00). There are lots of special events and several restaurants. The main restaurant serves a grand smorgasbord (135 kr). The Ekorren café offers the least-expensive self-service lunches with a view, but the Stora Gun-gan Krog (country inn) at the top of the escalator has better food (60 kr indoor or outdoor lunches with a salad bar).

Skansen is great for people-watching and picnicking, with open and covered benches all over (especially at Torslunden and Bollnastorget, where peacenik local toddlers don't bump on the bumper cars). Consider the 5 kr map or the 30 kr museum guidebook which has the same map, and check the live crafts schedule ("*Oppet I Hus Och Garder*," strangely in Swedish only) at the information stand at the top of the escalator or at Bollnastorget to confirm your Skansen plans.

Depart by the west entrance (Hazeliusporten) if you're heading for the Nordic Museum. Open May-August 9:00-22:00 (buildings 11:00-17:00); winter 9:00-17:00 (buildings 11:00-15:00). 50 kr entry, 30 kr in winter. (Bus #44, #47, or the Tourist Line, tel. 442-8250 for recorded schedule in Swedish, or 442-8000 for the day's tour, music, and dance schedule.) You can miss Grona Lund, the second-rate amusement park across the street.

▲▲▲**Vasa**—Stockholm turned a titanic flop into one of Scandinavia's great sightseeing attractions. This glamorous but unseaworthy warship sank 20 minutes into her 1628 maiden voyage. Top-heavy with a tacked on extra cannon deck, a breeze caught the sails and blew it over in the Stockholm harbor. After 333 years, it rose again from the deep (with the help of marine archaeologists), and today is the best-preserved ship of its kind anywhere, housed in a state-of-the-art museum. The masts on the roof are placed to show the actual size of the ship.

Catch the 25-minute English-subtitled movie (at the top of each hour, dubbed versions often play at 11:30 and 13:30), and for more information, take the free 25-minute

English tours (at the bottom of each hour from 10:30, every other hour off-season) to best enjoy and understand the ship. Learn about ship's rules (bread can't be older than 8 years), why it sank (heavy bread?), how it's preserved, and so on. Private tours are easy to freeload on, but the displays are so well described that a tour is hardly necessary. (45 kr, open daily mid-June to mid-August 9:30-19:00; off-season 10:00-17:00, winter on Wednesday until 20:00, tel. 666-4800). Take bus #44 or #47 just past the big brick Nordic Museum and catch the boat or walk from Skansen.

▲▲**Nordic Museum**—This museum, built to look like a Danish palace, offers a look at how Sweden lived over the last 500 years. Highlights include the Food and Drink section with its stunning china and crystal table settings, the Nordic folk art (second and third floors), the huge statue of Gustav Wasa, father of modern Sweden, by Carl Milles (top of second flight of stairs), and the Sami (Lapp) exhibit in the basement. (Open 11:00-17:00, Thursday until 20:00, closed Monday, tel. 666-4600). Worth your time if you have the Stockholm card, but it's over-priced at 50 kr admission. The 30 kr guidebook isn't necessary, but pick up the English brochure at the entrance.

▲**Thielska Galleriet**—If you liked the Larsson and Zorn art in the National Gallery and/or if you're a Munch fan, this charming mansion on the water at the far end of the Djur-garden park is worth the trip. (40 kr, Monday-Saturday 12:00-16:00, Sunday 13:00-16:00, tel. 662-5884, bus #69 from Karlaplan or boat from center).

▲**Sauna**—Sometime while you're in Sweden or Finland you'll have to treat yourself to Scandinavia's answer to support hose and a face lift. (A sauna is actually more Finnish than Swedish.) Simmer down with the local students, retired folks, and busy executives. Try to cook as calmly as the Swedes. Just before bursting, go into the shower room. There's no luke-cold, and the trickle down theory doesn't apply—only one button, bringing a Niagara of liquid ice. Suddenly your shower stall becomes a Cape Canaveral launch pad as your body scatters to every corner of the universe. A moment later you're back together. Rejoin the Swedes in the cooker, this time with their relaxed confidence; you now know that exhilaration is just around the corner. Only very rarely will you feel so good.

Any tourist office can point you toward the nearest birch twigs. Good opportunities include a Stockholm-Helsinki cruise, any major hotel you stay in (Hotel Karelia's is open to the public, 60 kr), some hostels, or least expensively, a public swimming pool. In Stockholm, consider the Eriksdalsbadet (Hammarby Slussvag 8, near Skanstull T-bana). Use of its 50-meter pool and first-rate sauna costs 30 kr.

The newly refurbished Centralbadet lets you enjoy an extensive gym, "bubblepool," sauna, steam room, and an elegant "art nouveau" pool from 1904 (70 kr, long hours, Drottningsgatan 88, 5 minutes up from Sergels Torg, tel. 24 24 03). Bring your towel into the sauna; the steam room is mixed, the sauna is not. Massage and solarium cost extra, and pool is more for floating than jumping and splashing. The leafy courtyard is an appropriately relaxing place to enjoy their restaurant (reasonable and healthy light meals).

Sights—Outer Stockholm

▲▲**Carl Milles Garden**—Here is the home housing the major work of Sweden's greatest sculptor, situated on a cliff overlooking Stockholm. Milles' entertaining, unique, and provocative art was influenced by Rodin. There's a classy café and a great picnic spot. T-bana to Ropsten, then take any bus to the first stop (Torsvik). It's a 5-minute walk from there (follow the signs). (40 kr, open daily 10:00-17:00, May-September; off-season Tuesday-Sunday 11:00-16:00, tel. 731-5060.)

▲**Drottningholm**—The queen's 17th-century summer castle and present royal residence has been called, not sur prisingly, Sweden's Versailles. It's great, but if you've seen Denmark's Frederiksborg Palace, skip it. The adjacent, uncannily well-preserved, baroque theater is the real high-light here, especially with its guided tours (30 kr, English theater tours twice an hour, May-September 12:00-16:30; in September 12:00-15:30). Get there by a pleasant, but over-priced, boat ride (55 kr round-trip, 2 hrs) or take the subway to Brommaplan and bus #301 or #323 to Drottningholm. (Palace and Theater open daily 11:00-16:30 May-August; in September daily 13:00-15:30, Saturday and Sunday 12:00-15:30, tel. 759-0310 for palace tours in English schedule often at 11:00, 30 kr.)

The 17th-century Drottningholm court theater performs perfectly authentic operas (about 30 performances each summer). Tickets to these very popular and unique shows go on sale each March. Prices for this time tunnel musical and theatrical experience are 60 kr-400 kr. For information, write (in February) to Drottningholm's Theater Museum, Box 27050, 10251 Stockholm, or phone 08/660-8281.

▲▲**Archipelago**—The world's most scenic islands (24,000 of them!) surround Stockholm. Europeans who spend entire vacations in and around Stockholm rave about them. If you cruise to Finland, you'll get a good 3-hour dose of this island beauty. Otherwise, consider the pleasant hour-long cruise (40 kr each way) from the Grand Hotel downtown to the quiet town of Vaxholm. The Tourist Office has a free Archipelago guide booklet.

Shopping

Modern design, glass, clogs, and wood goods are popular targets for shoppers. Browsing is a free, delightful way to enjoy Sweden's brisk pulse. Cop a feel at the Nordiska Kompaniet (NK, also meaning "no Kroner left") just across from the Sweden House or in the nearby Gallerian mall. The nearby Ahlens is less expensive. Swedish stores are open 9:30-18:00, until 14:00 on Saturday, and closed Sunday. Some of the bigger stores are open later on Saturday and on Sunday afternoon.

For fleas, visit the Loppmarknaden (northern Europe's biggest flea market) at the planned suburb of Skarholmen (10 kr, Monday-Friday 11:00-18:00, Saturday 9:00-15:00, Sunday 10:00-15:00, busiest on weekends, tel. 710-0060).

Sleeping in Stockholm
(7 kr = about $1, tel. code: 08)

Stockholm has plenty of money-saving deals for the savvy visitor. Its youth hostels are among Europe's best ($15 a bed) and plenty of people offer private accommodations ($50 doubles). Peak season for Stockholm's expensive hotels is business time—workdays outside of summer. Rates drop by 30 to 50 percent in the summer or on weekends, and, if business is slow, occasionally any night if you ask). To sort through all of this, the city has helpful, English-speaking room-finding services with handy locations and long hours. (See Hotell-centralen and Sweden House, above.)

The **Stockholm Package** offers business-class doubles with buffet breakfasts for 700 kr, includes two free Stockholm cards, and lets children up to 18 years old sleep for free. This is limited to mid-June to mid-August, and Friday and Saturday throughout the year. Assuming you'll be getting two Stockholm cards anyway (350 kr), this gives you a $200 hotel room for about $50. This is for real (summertime is that dead for business hotels). The procedure (through either tourist office) is easy: a 100 kr advance booking fee (you can arrange by fax, pay when you arrive) or a 40 kr in-person booking fee if you just drop in. Arriving without reservations in July is never a problem. It gets tight during the Water Festival (ten days in early August) and during a convention stretch for a few days in late June.

My listings are only a good value outside of Stockholm Package time, or if the 700 kr for a double and two cards is out of your range and you're hosteling. Every place listed here has staff who speak English and will explain their special deals to you on the phone. If money is limited, ask if they have cheaper rooms. It's not often that a hotel will push their odd misfit room that's 100 kr below all the others. And at any time of year, prices can be soft.

Sleep code: **S**=Single, **D**=Double/Twin, **T**=Triple, **Q**=Quad, **B**=Bath/Shower, **WC**=Toilet, **CC**=Credit Card (**V**isa, **M**astercard, **A**mex). "Summer rates" means mid-June to mid-August, and Friday and Saturday (sometimes Sunday) the rest of the year. Prices include breakfast unless otherwise noted.

Sleeping in Hotels

Queen's Hotel is cheery, clean, and just a 10-minute walk from the station, in a great pedestrian area across the street from the Centralbadet (city baths, listed on all maps). With a fine TV and piano lounge, coffee in the evenings, and a staff that enjoys its guests, this is probably the best cheap hotel in town (summer rates: D-435 kr, DB500 kr, DBWC-585 kr, 640 kr-845 kr in winter, CC:VMA, Drottninggatan 71A, tel. 24 94 60, fax 21 76 20).

Bentley's Hotel is an interesting option with an old English flair (summer rates include winter Sundays: small

DBWC-500 kr, DBWC-600 kr, suite DBWC-700 kr, CC:VMA, a block up the street from Queen's at Drottninggatan 77, 11160 Stockholm, tel. 14 13 95, fax 21 24 92) and a pile of decent but simple rooms with no sinks, plumbing, or breakfast (S-200 kr, D-400 kr). Klas and Agi Kallstrom are attempting to mix elegance, comfort, and simplicity into an affordable package. Each room is tastefully decorated with antique furniture, but has a modern full bathroom. Some rooms are no-smoking rooms.

Hotel Bema, also near the station, is modern, clean, and friendly. Ask for their weekend rate (even on a weekday) and eat pizza next door to save some money (DBWC-480 kr-727 kr depending on the season and day, CC:VMA, Upplandsgatan 13, S-11123 Stockholm, tel. 23 26 75, fax 20 53 38).

Hotel Karelia, a stately old Finnish-run hotel, is centrally located and a good value for a "normal" hotel (summer rates: small DBWC-670 kr, big DBWC-750 kr, but soft if they're really slow; winter rates: DBWC-1,100 kr, CC:VMA, swimming pool and sauna, 35 Birger Jarlsgatan, tel. 24 76 60, fax 24 15 11). They have 15 "cabin" rooms in the basement with no windows. These dark, elegantly wooden bunkbed doubles with modern full bathrooms are rented for 400 kr including their normal buffet breakfast (throughout the year except for a few convention weeks). For the right vagabond, traveling in "high" season, these are a great deal.

Hotel Ostermalm (summer rates: no sink D-290 kr, DBWC-340 kr-460 kr, DBWC suite/family room-490 kr, 120 kr-150 kr for extra beds, 60 kr per double, less without breakfast, pricing here seems arbitrary and banana-firm, elevator, Karlavagen 57, tel. 660-6996, tel./fax 661-0471) is in a simple stately building a block from the T-bahn: Stadion. Narrow, yellow halls connect its generally huge (formerly elegant but now a tad musty) rooms. A funkiness rare in Stockholm, and for the right traveler a ripe deal. Nearby, the proud little **Stureparkens Gastvaning** (summer rates: no sink D-450 kr; high season: no sink D-600 kr, 2-night minimum, CC:VM, elevator, Sturegatan 58, tel. 662-7230, fax 661-5713) is a carefully run, traditional-feeling place with lots of class and ten tastefully decorated rooms. Its a better value during the high season.

Hotel Anno 1647, a typical old Swedish hotel with a few showerless rooms, just off the Old Town near Slussen (under the Katarina elevator), is a good splurge (summer rates, including Sunday through the year: D-500 kr, DBWC-750 kr; high season: D-650 kr, CC:VMA, Mariagrand 3, tel. 644-0480, fax 643-3700).

Sleeping in Rooms in Private Homes

Stockholm's centrally-located private rooms are as expensive as cheap hotels—a deal only in the high season. More reasonable rooms are a few T-bana minutes from the center. Stockholm's tourist offices refer those in search of a room in a private house to Hoteljanst (near the station, at Vasagatan 15, tel. 10 44 67, fax 21 37 16). They can set you up for about 330 kr per double, minimum two nights. Go direct—you'll save your host the listing service's fee. Be sure to get the front door security code when you call, as there's no intercom connection with front doors.

Mrs. Lindstrom rents out three doubles in her comfortable home (D-300 kr with access to a kitchenette, Danavagen 39, tel. 37 16 08, in the Bromma district near the Drottningholm Palace, a 7-minute walk from T-bana: Islandstorget).

Else Mari Sundin (D-400 kr with breakfast, bus #47 or #69 to Torstenssonsgatan 7, go through courtyard to "garden house" and up to second floor, tel. 665-3348, or at her country home, 036/45151) is an effervescent retired actress who rents two rooms in her very homey place, beautifully located just two blocks from the bridge to Djurgarden.

Mrs. Lichtsteiner (DBWC-400 kr without breakfast but with kitchenette, also a family room with a loft, a block from T-bahn: Radhuset, exit T-bahn direction Polisehusit, at Bergsgatan 45, inside go through door on left and up elevator to second floor, tel. 746-9166) will have you singing, "We represent the Lollipop Guild."

Sleeping in Youth Hostels

Stockholm has Europe's best selection of hostels offering good beds in simple but interesting places for 90 kr. If your budget is tight, these are right. Each has a helpful English-speaking staff, pleasant family rooms, good facilities, and good leads on budget survival in Stockholm. All will hold rooms for a phone call. Hosteling is cheap only if you're a member (guest membership: 35 kr a night necessary only in IYHF places), bring your own sheet (paper sheets rent for 30 kr), and picnic for breakfast (breakfasts cost 40 kr). Several of the hostels are often booked up well in advance, but hold a few beds for those who are left in the lurch.

Af Chapman (IYHF)—Europe's most famous youth hostel is the permanently moored cutter ship *Af Chapman*. Just a 5-minute walk from downtown, this floating hostel has 140 beds—2-8 per stateroom. A popular but compassionate place, it's often booked far in advance, but saves some beds each morning for unreserved arrivals. If you call at breakfast time and show up before 12:00, you may land a bed, even in summer. A warm, youthful atmosphere prevails. Study the warden's personal scrapbook of budget Stockholm information (April to mid-December, 7:00-12:00, 15:00-02:00, sleeping bags allowed, with a lounge and cafeteria that welcomes non-hostelers, 12:00-18:00, STF Vandrarhem *Af Chapman*, Skeppsholmen, 11149 Stockholm, tel. 679-5015).

Skeppsholmen Hostel (IYHF)—Just ashore from the *Af Chapman*, this hostel is open all year. It has better facilities and smaller rooms (90 kr per bed in doubles, triples, and quads, only 60 kr in dorms, tel. 679-5017), but it isn't as romantic as its sea-going sister. If you're staying in a hostel on Skeppsholmen island, the neighboring Sommar Café has a laundromat.

Zinken Hostel (IYHF)—This is a big, basic hostel in a busy suburb (T-bana: Zinkensdamm) with plenty of doubles, a launderette, and the best hostel kitchen facilities in town. (STF Vandrarhcm Zinken, Zinkens Vag 20, tel. 668-5786, open 24 hours, all year.) If you want a 180 kr double (extra for sheets and non-members), sleep here. A great no-nonsense user-friendly value.

Vandrarhemmet Brygghuset—This former brewery near Odenplan (open June-August 7:00-12:00, 15:00-23:00, no curfew, Norrtullsgatan 12 N, tel. 312424) is small (57 beds in 12 rooms), spacious, bright and clean, quiet, with a laundromat and a kitchen. Since this is a private hostel, its 2- to 6-bed rooms are open to all for 110 kr per bed (no sleeping bags allowed, sheets rent for 30 kr). Doubles are 300 kr.

Café Bed and Breakfast, is Stockholm's newest cozy hostel with only 30 beds (110 kr per bed in 8- to 12-bed rooms, 30 kr for breakfast, 30 kr for sheets, near Radmansgatan T-bana stop, Rehnsgatan 21, tel. 15 28 38). They have three 300 kr doubles. Note: used sheets are rented for 10 kr ("locals don't mind").

Camping—Stockholm has seven campgrounds (located south of town) that are a wonderful solution to your parking and budget problems. The TI's "Camping Stockholm" brochure has specifics.

Eating in Stockholm

Stockholm's elegant department stores (notably NK and Ahlens near Sergelstorg) have cafeterias for the kroner-pinching local shopper. Look for the 50 kr "rodent of the day" (*Dagens ratt*) specials. Most museums have handy cafés. The café at the **Af Chapman youth hostel** (open to the public daily 12:00-18:00) serves a good salad/roll/coffee lunch in an unbeatable deck-of-a-ship atmosphere (if the weather's good).

In the Old Town (Gamla Stan), don't miss the wonderfully atmospheric **Kristina Restaurang** (Vesterlanggatan 68, Gamla Stan, tel. 200529). In this 1632 building, under a leather ceiling steeped in a turn-of-the-century interior, you'll find good dinners from 110 kr, including a salad and cracker bar. (The delicious Swedish meatballs with lingonberries is one of the least expensive meals.) They serve a great 50 kr lunch (11:00-15:30)—entrée, salad bar, bread, and drink. The place is best Wednesday-Saturday 20:00-23:00, when live jazz accompanies your meal (silent in July). You can enjoy the music over just a beer or coffee, too.

Picnics

With higher taxes almost every year, Sweden's restaurant industry is suffering. You'll notice many fine places almost empty. Swedes joke that the local cuisine is now Chinese, Italian, and hamburgers. Here more than anywhere, budget travelers should picnic.

Stockholm's major department stores (and the many small corner groceries) are fine places to assemble a picnic. Ahlens department store (near Sergels Torg, open until

21:00) has a great food section. The late-hours supermarket downstairs in the central train station (Monday-Friday 7:00-23:00, Saturday and Sunday 9:00-23:00) is picnic-friendly with fresh ready-made sandwiches.

The market at **Hotorget** is a fun place to picnic shop, especially in the indoor, exotic ethnic Hotorgshallen. The outdoor market closes at 18:00, and many merchants put their unsold produce on the push list (earlier closing and more desperate merchants on Saturday).

For a classy vegetarian buffet lunch (65 kr, Monday-Friday until 17:00) or dinner (75 kr, evenings and weekends) often with a lunchtime piano serenade, eat at **Ortagarden** (literally "the herb garden," Nybrogatan 31, tel. 662-1728), above the colorful old Ostermalms food market at Ostermalmstorg.

Transportation Connections

Stockholm to: Copenhagen (6/day, 8 hrs), **Oslo** (3/day, 7 hrs), **Kalmar** (6/day 8 hrs), **Uppsala** (30/day, 45 min), **Helsinki** (daily/nightly boats, 14 hrs, for detailed info, see Helsinki chapter), **Turku** (daily/nightly boats, 10 hrs). Estline runs a regular ferry from Stockholm to **Tallinn, Estonia** (every other night at 17:30, arriving at 9:00 the next morning, 385 kr each way). They offer a 36-hour tour (no visa necessary, round-trip, simple 2-bed cabins, two breakfasts, two dinners) for 1,170 kr per person (tel. 08/667-0001).

Uppsala

Uppsala is a compact and bustling little city with a cathedral and university that win "Sweden's oldest/largest/tallest" awards. While not of great touristic importance, Uppsala has a lot of history, and if you want a look at small-town Sweden, this is a handy place to start. Uppsala could absorb the better part of a day, including the frequent train connection from Stockholm.

The sights of historic Uppsala, along with its 30,000 students, cluster around the university and cathedral. Just over the river is the bustling shopping center and pedestrian zone. The tourist office has a branch near the cathedral (Monday-Friday 10:00-18:00, Saturday 10:00-15:00, Sunday 12:00-16:00, shorter hours off-season) and one in the castle (daily in summer, tel. 018/274800). Pick up their free entertaining and helpful Uppsala guide.

Sights—Uppsala

▲▲**Uppsala Cathedral**—One of Scandinavia's largest and most historic cathedrals has a breathtaking interior, the tomb of King Gustavus Vasa, and twin 400-foot spires. Ask about a guided tour. Otherwise, push the English button, sit down, and listen to the tape-recorded introduction in the narthex opposite the tourist information table (daily June-August 8:00-20:00, off-season until 18:00).

The University—Scandinavia's first university was founded here in 1477. Linnaeus and Celsius are two famous grads. Several of the old buildings are open to guests. A very historic (but not much to see) old silver-bound Gothic Bible is on display with many other rare medieval books in the Carolina Rediviva (library). The anatomy theater in the Gustavianum is thought-provoking. This strange theater's only show was a human dissection.

Gamla Uppsala—Old Uppsala is rooted deeply in history, but now almost entirely lost in the sod of centuries. Look at the postcards of Gamla Uppsala's 15 grassy burial mounds from downtown. That's all you'll see if you go out there. Easy by car, not worth the headache by bus (#20, #24, or #54).

Other Uppsala Sights—The free (and cute) little **Uppland Museum** is on the river by the waterfall (daily 12:00-17:00). Nearby is the **Carl Linnaeus Garden and Museum** and the 16th-century castle (with its slice of castle life exhibits) on the hilltop overlooking the town.

Eating in Uppsala

Browse through the lively **Saluhallen**, the riverside indoor market in the shadow of the cathedral. You'll find great picnic stuff and pleasant cafés. This entire university district abounds with inexpensive eateries. Try **Kung Kral** by the river and cathedral for great food and a special five-shot sampler of Scandinavian snaps for the brave (St. Persgata 4, tel. 018/12 50 90).

Sigtuna

Between Stockholm and Uppsala you'll pass Sigtuna. Possibly Sweden's cutest town, Sigtuna is basically fluff. You'll see a medieval lane lined with colorful wooden tourist shops, a very pleasant tourist office with a reading room, a café, a romantic park, a promenade along the lake, an old church, and some rune stones. The TI organizes walking tours in English (summer afternoons at 13:15). If it's sunny, Sigtuna is worth a browse and an ice cream cone, but little more.

Route Tips for Drivers

Stockholm to Oslo: From downtown, follow Sveavegen west and signs to Nortull/Gottberg/E-3/E-4 south. Take the second E-18 you see (immediately after the first). From Uppsala to Oslo, it's about 325 miles. That's 7 hours of mostly clear freeway motoring. Leaving Uppsala, follow signs for Route 55 and Norrkoping. When you hit E-18, just follow the Oslo signs past forests, lakes, and prettily painted wooden houses. It's pleasant, but I'd stop only to fill and empty the tanks. (Or maybe at one of the many Lopp-markets, flea markets, you may see advertised or at Ester's Cafe, on the right just before Arjang.)

You'll also pass several youth hostel signs (the house and tree indicates 90 kr dorm beds). The town of **Arjang**, just before the Norwegian border, is a good place to stop if you don't make it to Oslo. The Argang TI (tel. 0573/14136, open 9:00-20:00, less on weekends and off-season) books private rooms (D-220 kr plus a 50 kr fee). **Hotel Karl XII** offers the cheapest hotel beds (all year D-300 kr without breakfast, Sveavagen #22, near marketplace, tel. 0573/10156, fax 711426).

There are no border formalities, unless you've got a tax refund to process for something you bought duty-free in Sweden. At the border, change money at the bank desk at the little TI kiosk (left side of road under flags, daily summer 10:00-19:00, fair rates, standard 20 kr per traveler's check or cash fee). If you change a traveler's check you can convert your extra Swedish paper and coins for no extra fee. Call to reconfirm your Oslo hotel, and pick up the free Oslo map and *What's On* publication.

The ride from the border to Oslo is particularly scenic. The freeway dumps you right into downtown Oslo. Just follow the E-18 signs to Sentrum, then Sentral Stasjon and Paleet P. If you're going directly to a room on the west end, keep left following signs to Oslo V, veering right toward the palace immediately after passing the harborfront and twin brick towers of the city hall. If your hotel is in the center near the station, don't take the Sentrum O exit, instead follow the sign for Paleet P. (At the Paleet P parking garage, turn right on Fred Olsens Gate, a block and a half for the Sjomannshjem.)

For driving from Kalmar and the south into Stockholm, see Route Tips for Drivers in the next chapter, South Sweden.

SOUTH SWEDEN: VAXJO AND KALMAR

Outside of Stockholm, the most interesting region in Sweden is Smaland. This Swedish province is famous for its forests, lakes, great glass, and the many emigrants it sent to the U.S.A. More Americans came from this area than any other part of Scandinavia, and the immigration center in Vaxjo tells the story well. Between Vaxjo and Kalmar is Glass Country, a 70-mile stretch of forest sparkling with glassworks. Of the prestigious glassworks that welcome curious visitors, Kosta's is best. Historic Kalmar has a rare Old World ambience and the most magnificent medieval castle in Scandinavia. From Kalmar, you can cross Europe's longest bridge to hike through the Stonehenge-type mysteries of the strange island of Oland.

Planning Your Time

By train, on a 3-week Scandinavian trip, I'd skip this area in favor of the slick night train from Copenhagen to Stockholm (and a side trip to Estonia). If you're driving, the sights described below make that same trip an interesting way to spend a couple of days. You'll gather that—and this has only a little to do with my Norwegian heritage—I'm not so hot on the Swedish countryside. Still, you can't only see Stockholm and say you've seen Sweden. Vaxjo and Kalmar give you the best possible dose of small-town and country-side Sweden. (I find Lund and Malmo, both popular side trips from Copenhagen, really dull. And I'm not old enough to find a sleepy trip along the much-loved Gota Canal appealing.) Drivers spend 3 days getting from Copenhagen to Stockholm this way:

Day 1: Leave Copenhagen after breakfast, tour Frederiksborg Castle, picnic under the Kronborg castle; take the 14:00 ferry to Sweden, drive northeast; at 18:00 set up in Vaxjo.

Day 2: Tour Vaxjo's Smalands folk museum and Emigrants Center, drive into glass country, tour the Kosta glassworks (or the smaller more traditional Bergdala works); at 14:30 set up in Kalmar in time to tour the castle and its provincial museum; evening in Kalmar.

Day 3: At 8:00 begin 5-hour drive north along the coast to Stockholm; at 10:30 break in Vastervik; at 12:00 stop in Soderkoping for a picnic lunch and a walk along the Gota Canal; at 13:30 continue drive north; and at 16:00 arrive in Stockholm and possibly catch the night boat to Helsinki.

Thinking ahead to your Helsinki cruise: boat tickets may be cheaper (off-weekend) and your drive to Oslo more reasonable (earlier start) if you do the Helsinki excursion immediately after Kalmar, before seeing Stockholm.

South Sweden: Vaxjo and Kalmar

Vaxjo

A pleasant but rather dull town of 50,000, Vaxjo (veh-quah, the Swedish "xj" is like our "qu") is in the center of Smaland. A stroll through downtown Vaxjo is perhaps the purest Swedish experience you can have.

Orientation (tel. code: 0470)

The town is compact, with the train station, town square, two important museums, and the tourist office all within 2 blocks of each other. Vaxjo has an easy-to-enjoy pedestrian center, and the nearby lake is encircled by a pleasant 3-mile path.

Tourist Information

On the main square (Kronobergsgatan 8, tel. 0470/41410 or 41000, open July to mid-August Monday-Friday 9:00-18:00, Saturday 10:00-14:00, closed Sunday; May and mid-August to September Monday-Friday 9:00-17:00; winter Monday-Friday 10:00-15:00).

Helpful Hints

A farmers' market bustles on the main square on Wednesday and Saturday mornings. The bank across from the train station opens at 9:00.

Sights—Vaxjo

▲House of Emigrants—A large part of the 1,300,000 Swedes who moved to the U.S.A. came from this neck of the Swedish woods. If you have Swedish roots, this place is really exciting. If not, its small exhibit is mildly interesting. The Dream of America exhibit tells the story of the 1850s-1920s "American Fever." (The emigration festival, 3 days around the second Sunday in August, is a real hoot, as thousands of Minnesotans storm Vaxjo.)

Upstairs is an excellent library and research center (you're welcome to take a peek). Root-seekers (10,000 a year from the U.S.) are very welcome. Advance notice is urged (write well in advance to Box 20l, S-351 04, Vaxjo, for research form and information) and bring what information you have—such as ship names and birthdays. (25 kr, open Monday-Friday 9:00-17:00, Saturday 11:00-15:00, Sunday 13:00-17:00, shorter hours off-season, tel. 0470/20l20, the research center is open Monday-Thursday 9:00-16:00, Friday 9:00-12:00, 50 kr per half-day.) The Liv Ullman movie about the cmigration called *The Immigrants*, and its sequel, *The New Land*, are great pre-trip viewing.

▲Smalands Museum—This cute small-townish museum (one of Sweden's oldest) offers a good look at local forestry, a prehistoric exhibit, a wonderful traditional costume display (top floor), and most important, an introduction to the area's glass industry with the best glass collection around. They've promised to label things in English. If not, there's a free, helpful English brochure. (20 kr, Monday-Friday 9:00-16:00, Saturday 11:00-15:00, Sunday 13:00-17:00, just next to the Emigrants House and worth more time.)

Cathedral—Vaxjo's fine cathedral (dedicated to the 11th-century English missionary, Saint Sigfrid) offers free summer concerts, many Thursday evenings at 20:00.

Linneparken—This lovely park, behind the cathedral, is dedicated to the great Swedish botanist, Carl von Linne (a.k.a. Carolus Linnaeus). It has an arboretum, lots of well-categorized perennials, and a big children's playground.

Swimming pool—From the Emigrants Museum you can see the town's super-modern lakeside swimming hall (Simhall) a 5-minute walk away (25 kr including the sauna, plus a little more if you want to tan or use the exercise room, towels 5 kr, daily until 19:00 or 21:00, tel. 41204).

Sleeping in Vaxjo
(7 kr = about $1, tel. code: 0470)
Sleep code: **S**=Single, **D**=Double/Twin, **T**=Triple, **Q**=Quad, **B**=Bath/Shower, **WC**=Toilet, **CC**=Credit Card (Visa, Mastercard, Amex). Rates include breakfast.

Sleeping in Hotels and Motels
Hotel Esplanad is your best central hotel value (summer rates: D-350 kr, DBWC-420 kr; high-season rates: D-520 kr, DBWC-690 kr, CC:VM, Esplanad 21A, 352 31 Vaxjo, tel. 22580, fax 26226). From the freeway, follow "centrum" signs into town. At the Royal Corner Hotel, turn left, 200 yards later, at the first light, turn right onto Esplanade. The yellow hotel is on the right. This quiet and comfortable old hotel, run by Birgit, is just 3 blocks from the town center.

Sara Hotel Statt, in the town center, is more traditional, and borderline luxurious (DBWC-1300 kr; summer rate: DBWC-750 kr, CC:VMA, 6 Kungsgatan, tel. 13400, fax 44837).

Kinnevaldsgardens Motel is a homey place run by Eva and Lasse Andersson (and their four young children) like a British B&B (S-220 kr, D-350 kr). They are generous with maps, information, and evening cake and coffee. Just outside of town, leave the freeway on the Morners Vag exit, and turn in the direction of Ojaby; it's across the street from the Q-8 gas station. Or take bus #4 (10 kr) from the station in Vaxjo (St. Vagen 9, Bergsnas, tel. 60887).

Sleeping in Rooms in Private Homes

For a 25 kr fee, the tourist office can always find private rooms for 140 kr per person, 115 kr if you have sheets. Breakfast is usually 30 kr extra. To save money and be assured of a good value, go or call direct to the following places.

Eva and Hakan Edfeldt are a young professional couple with two boys who live in a woodsy 80-year-old house in a folksy old neighborhood (1 double and 1 triple, kitchenette, 8-minute walk from the station, take the bridge over the tracks, follow Varendsgatan to the lake, at Skanegaten turn right, Skanegaten ends at the Edfeldt's driveway, Telestadsgatan 6, 35235 Vaxjo, tel. 0470/19242 or during the day at their work tel. 88000). The whole family speaks great English. **Siv Kidvik**, a more comfortable, newer home run by an older couple, is fine for families with a car and has a great garden (4 rooms only, May-August, kitchenette, children half price). Drive north from the center on Linnegatan which becomes Sandsbrovagen. At the end of the cemetery before the Shell Tankomat station, go right on Lillestadsvagen, take the first left onto Gamla Norrvagen, then the first left onto Kastanjevagen to #70 Kastanjevagen (tel. 17053, speak slowly and clearly).

Sleeping in the Youth Hostel

Vaxjo has a fine **youth hostel** on a lake, 2 miles out of town (STF Vandrarhem Evedal—IYHF, 35590 Vaxjo, tel. 63070, open 8:00-10:00, 18:00-21:00, 2- to 4-bed rooms, 90 kr beds, 40 kr breakfast, 35 kr extra for non-members, telephone reservations required in summer). Take bus #1C from the tourist office to the last stop (summer only, last ride 18:15, first ride 10:00, so hitch a ride into Vaxjo with a fellow hosteler).

Eating in Vaxjo

For reasonable eating in downtown Vaxjo, try **La Gondola** (corner of Storgatan and Liedbergsgatan, open nightly until midnight, plenty of 50 kr Italian-style meals (great lasagna) with a salad bar, tel. 27632), **McDonald's** (on Storgatan), **Ahlens Supermarket** (on Storgatan, open Monday-Friday until 19:00, cheap fried chicken for a classier dinner picnic), **Spisen** (more expensive Swedish food, across from the station), or the **fish and chips kiosk** next to the train station.

Those at the hostel can buy a picnic dinner at the neighboring campground's little store.

Transportation Connections
Copenhagen to Vaxjo (6/day with a change in Alvesta, 5 hrs), **Vaxjo to Kalmar** (9/day, 1¹/₂ hrs), **Kalmar to Stockholm** (6/day, 8 hrs). While there are **bus** connections from Vaxjo to Kosta and organized **bus tours** of the glass country from Vaxjo, the glassworks aren't really worth the trouble, unless you have a car. Instead, I'd take a careful look at the glass exhibit in the Vaxjo museum and train straight to Kalmar.

Sights—Between Vaxjo and Kalmar
Lessebo Papermill—The little town of Lessebo has a 300-year-old paper mill that's kept working for visitors to see. If you've never seen handmade paper produced, this mill is free and worth a visit. Pick up the English brochure. (7:00-16:00 Monday-Friday, tours in English at 9:30, 10:30, 13:00 and 14:15 in summer, the mill makes paper 7:00-11:15, 12:30-15:30, otherwise it's open but dead, tel. 0478/10600.) If you're driving, Lessebo is an easy stop between Vaxjo and Kosta. Just after the Kosta turnoff, you'll see a black-and-white Handpapersbruk sign.

▲▲**The Kingdom of Crystal**—This is Sweden's Glass Country. Frankly, these glassworks cause so much excitement because of the relative rarity of anything else thrilling in Sweden outside of greater Stockholm. Pick up the Glasriket Kingdom of Crystal brochure in Vaxjo or Kalmar. The following three glassworks give tours and welcome visitors. Orrefors is most famous; Bergdala is cutest; Kosta treats its tourists best.

   Bergdala has a glassworks that offers a fine close-up look at actual craftsmen blowing and working the red-hot glass, a good shop (with Bergdala's tempting blue-ringed cereal bowls), and a fine picnic area with covered tables if it's wet. (30 min east of Vaxjo, exit road 25 at Bergdala sign, drive 3 miles north; open 9:00-14:30, Saturday 10:00-15:00, Sunday 12:00-16:00, no action 12:00-12:30, tel. 0478/11650).

   Kosta is your best major glassworks stop. This town boasts the oldest of the glasbruks, dating back to 1742. Today, the glassworks is a thriving tourist and shopping center (open year-round 9:00-18:00, Saturday 10:00-16:00, Sunday 12:00-16:00; tours on the hour leaving 11:00-14:00; actual glass-blowing is seen only on work days but not from 10:00-11:00, tel. 0478/50300, Diana Hansen is a great guide). On arrival, report to the information desk to get your English tour. Tours start in the historic and glass display rooms, then go to the actual blowing room where guides are constantly narrating the ongoing work.

Kosta is making great strides toward lead-free crystal; their crystal is already 80 percent lead-free. Visitors show the most enthusiasm in the shopping hall, where crystal "seconds" and discontinued models are sold at very good prices. This is duty-free shopping and they'll happily mail your purchases home. Kosta's best picnic tables (rainproof) are at the Gamla Kosta museum. Kosta is a well-signposted 15-minute drive from Lessebo. In town, follow signs for Glasbruk.

Orrefors has the most famous of the several renowned glassworks in Glass Country, but its glassworks are quite a tourist racket and offer lousy tours (tel. 0481/34000 to confirm tour times). Most visitors just observe the work from platforms. Like Kosta, their shop sells nearly perfect crystal seconds at deep discounts. (Open July Monday-Friday 9:00-18:00, Saturday 9:00-16:00, Sunday 11:00-16:00; off-season closes an hour earlier.) Don't miss the dazzling "museum" (open same hours as shop).

Kalmar

Kalmar feels formerly strategic and important. In its day, Kalmar was called the gateway to Sweden. Today, it's just a sleepy has-been, and gateway only to the holiday island of Oland. Kalmar's salty old center, fine castle, and busy waterfront give it a wistful sailor's charm. The town is wonderfully walkable.

Orientation (tel. code: 0480)
Kalmar's summer is from about mid-June to mid-August.

Tourist Information
The Kalmar Tourist Office is central and helpful (Larmgatan 6, tel. 0480/15350, open mid-June to mid-August Monday-Friday 9:00-21:00, Saturday 9:00-17:00, Sunday 12:00-18:00;

closing at 17:00 other months and closed on winter weekends). Get the handy town map and confirm your sightseeing plans. For train connections, see above under Vaxjo.

Kalmar

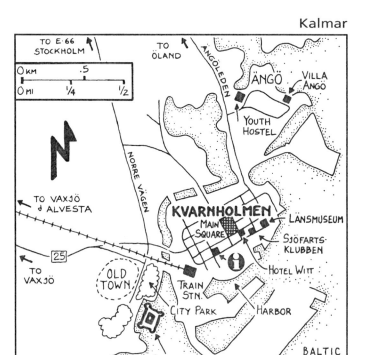

Sights—Kalmar

▲▲**Kalmar Castle**—This moated castle is one of Europe's great medieval experiences. The stark exterior, cuddled by a lush park, houses a fine Renaissance palace interior, which is the work of King Gustavus Vasa. The elaborately furnished rooms are entertainingly explained in English, and a more extensive guidebook is available for 20 kr. Notice how the electric candles "flicker" (40 kr, open mid-June to mid-August 10:00-18:00, Sunday 12:00-18:00; shoulder season 12:00-18:00; November-March much shorter hours, tel. 56351.)

▲▲**Kalmar Provincial (Lans) Museum**—This museum displays the impressive salvaged wreck of the royal ship *Kronan*, which sank nearby in 1676. Lots of interesting soggy bits and old pieces with a here's-the-buried-treasure thrill, but unfortunately no information in English. (You can borrow the Kronan exhibit in English text). See the excellent 12-minute English film (request an English showing as you enter). It's right downtown on the waterfront. (30 kr, open mid-June to mid-August, 10:00-18:00, Sunday 12:00-16:00, off-season closes at 16:00, tel. 56300.)

▲**The Island of Oland**—Europe's longest bridge (4 miles, free) connects Oland with Kalmar and the mainland. The island, 90 miles long and only 8 miles wide, is a pleasant local resort known for its birds, windmills, flowers, beaches, and prehistoric sights. Public transportation is miserable and the island is only worthwhile if you have a car and 3 extra hours. A 60-mile circle south of the bridge will give you a good dose of the island's windy rural charm.

The **Gettlinge Gravfalt** (just off the road about 10 miles up from the south tip) is a wonderfully situated boat-shaped Iron Age grave site littered with monoliths, overseen by a couple of creaky old windmills. It offers a commanding view of the windy and mostly treeless island.

Farther south is the **Eketorp Prehistoric Fort**, a very reconstructed fifth-century stone fort that, as Iron Age forts go, is fairly interesting. Several evocative huts and buildings are filled with what someone imagines may have been the style back then, and the huge rock fort is surrounded by strange, runty pig-like creatures that were common 1,500 years ago. A sign reads: "For your convenience and pleasure, don't leave your children alone with the animals." (40 kr, open daily May to mid-September 9:00-17:00, free English tours usually at 13:00 in summer, tel. 0485/62023.)

Sleeping in Kalmar
(7 kr = about $1, tel. code: 0480)
The tourist office can always find you a room in a private home (220 kr per double, 40 kr per person for sheets, and a 40 kr per booking fee, no breakfast). They can also get you special last-minute discounts on fancy hotels.

Sleep code: **S**=Single, **D**=Double/Twin, **T**=Triple, **Q**=Quad, **B**=Bath/Shower, **WC**=Toilet, **CC**=Credit Card (**V**isa, **M**astercard, **A**mex).

A 15-minute walk from the center, you'll find a wonderful **IYHF hostel** and hotel annex run by Torsten Knutsson and family. The hostel has 2- or 4-bed rooms, laundry, TV, and sauna (40 kr/hr per couple, 90 kr per bed, 35 kr for sheets, 35 kr without hostel card, 38 kr breakfast, closed 10:00-16:30). Try the hotel annex, the **Kalmar Lagprishotell Svanen** (S-275 kr, D-395 kr including sheets and breakfast, STF Vandrarhem, Rappegatan 1, 39230 Kalmar, tel. 25560, fax 88293.) You'll see a blue-and-white hotel sign and hostel symbol at the edge of town on Angoleden Street, less than a mile from the train station.

Sjofartsklubben (Seaman's Club)—In June, July, and August, Mr. Persson, who speaks only a little English, opens his clean, salty, dorm to tourists. (It's the home of student sailors during the school year.) He has 1- to 5-bed rooms with kitchen privileges and a lively common room. At 100 kr per person, plus 40 kr for sheets with a garden facing the harbor, this has, by far, the best cheap beds in Kalmar (Olandsgatan 45, tel. 10810).

Soderportsgarden is a university dorm that opens up mid-June to mid-August for tourists (D-400 kr including sheets and breakfast, Slottsvagen 1, tel. 12501). It's beautifully located next to a park, directly in front of the castle.

Hotel Villa Ango—A big old house on the water, a 10-minute walk out of town, has a price that fluctuates with its erratic management (D400 kr-600 kr with breakfast in summer, Bagensgatan 20, tel. 85415).

Stadts Hotel (summer rate: DBWC-600 kr, CC:VMA, very central at Stortorget 14, tel. 15180, fax 15847) is a 1,200 kr place with an affordable summer price.

Eating in Kalmar

Bistro Matisse (1 Kaggensgatan) offers a delicious inexpensive lunch. The **Domus Department Store** (2 blocks off the town square on the pedestrian street) has a ground-floor café with cheap sandwich-type meals. Upstairs, its **4 Kok** cafeteria serves reasonable meals. This is the place for evening picnic dinner shopping (open daily until 20:00, café and cafeteria until 19:00). Pizza, Chinese food, salad bars, **Kalmar Hamkrog** for fish on the harbor, or the café in the Stroget mall (just off Storgatan) are also good budget bets.

Byttan Restaurant—For a splurge, in a venerable old restaurant with music on many summer evenings, head out to the castle to enjoy a great waterfront terrace and a 120 kr meal or memorable cup of coffee.

Route Tips for Drivers

For Copenhagen to Sweden, including the Helsingor ferry information, see Route Tips for Drivers at the end of the Copenhagen chapter.

From Helsingborg to Vaxjo to Kalmar to Stockholm: In Helsingborg follow signs for E-4 and Stockholm. The road's good, traffic's light, and towns are all clearly signposted. You'll make good time. At Ljungby, road 25 takes you to Vaxjo and Kalmar. Entering Vaxjo, skip the first Vaxjo exit and follow the freeway into "centrum" where it ends.

The 70-mile drive from Vaxjo to Kalmar is a joy—light traffic and endless forest and lake scenery punctuated by numerous glassworks (*glasbruk*). The free TI "Kingdom of Crystal" glass country map lists them all and is your best navigational tool. Leave Vaxjo on road 25 to Kalmar. The driving time between Vaxjo and Kosta is 45 minutes; between Kosta and Kalmar, 45 minutes.

Kalmar to **Vastervik** (90 min) to **Soderkoping** (60 min) to **Stockholm** (3 hrs): Leaving Kalmar, follow the E-22 Lindsdal and Norrkoping signs. The Kalmar-Stockholm drive is 240 miles and takes about 5 hours. Sweden did a cheap widening job, paving the shoulders of the old two-lane road to get about 3.8 lanes. Still, the traffic is polite and sparse. There's little to see or do, so stock the pantry, set the compass on north, and home in on Stockholm. (You won't see Stockholm signs until after Norrkoping.)

Make two pleasant stops along the way. Ninety miles north is Vastervik, with a pleasant 18th-century core of wooden houses (3 miles off the highway, centrum signs lead you to the harbor, park at the little salty, six-days-a-week-and-great-smoked-fish market on the waterfront next to the seven-days-a-week, picnic-perfect Exet supermarket and a public WC).

Soderkoping is just right for a lunch on the Gota Canal stop. Stay on E-22 past the town center, turn right at the TI/Kanalbatarna/Slussen/Kanal P signs. Park by the canal, 1 block toward the hill from the town square and TI.

Sweden's famous Gota Canal is 110 miles of lakes and canals cutting Sweden in half with 58 locks (*slussen*) working slowly up to a summit of 300 feet. It was built 150 years ago, with more than 7 million 12-hour man-days (60,000 men working about 22 years) at a low ebb in the country's self-esteem—to show her industrial oats. Today, it's a lazy 3- or 4-day tour for experts in lethargy. We'll just take a quick peak at the Gota Canal over lunch, as it passes through the medieval town of Soderkoping.

The TI on Soderkoping's Radhustorget (a square about a block off the canal) has good English town maps and canal information (pick up a map of Stockholm if you don't have one). From there go to the canal. The Toalett sign points to the Kanulbatiquen, a yachters' laundry (wash and dry, 40 kr, open every day), shower, shop, and WC with idyllic canalside picnic tables just over the lock. Munch down. From the lock a series of stairs leads up to the Utsiktsplats pavilion (a nice view, but not quite worth the hike unless you need the exercise).

Leaving Soderkoping, E-22 takes you to Norrkoping, where you'll get lost unless you follow the E-4 signs winding through Norrkoping, then past a handy over-the-freeway rest stop into Stockholm. Stockholm's centrum is clearly marked. (The Viking ferry terminal for Helsinki is in Sodermalm.)

HELSINKI

Finland
Finland is the odd duck in this book, and as such it deserves special comment. First, a brief history lesson.

History
As far as the sightseer is concerned, Finland's history breaks into three parts: Swedish (before the 1809 Russian takeover, because of city fires, very little remains physically), Russian (1809-1917, when most of Helsinki's great buildings were built), and independent (when Finland's bold, trend-setting modern design and architecture blossomed). After World War II, Finland teetered between independence and the U.S.S.R., treading very lightly on matters concerning her fragile autonomy and relations with her giant neighbor to the east. The recent collapse of the U.S.S.R. has done to Finland what a good long sauna might do to you.

Lately, unemployment and a high cost of living have been Finland's main problems. The average income is about $30,000—with about 35 percent going to taxes. About 70 percent of the people rent apartments that can be had in Helsinki for about $800 a month including heat.

Weather
They say the people of Finland spend nine months in winter and the other three months waiting for summer. The weather dictates a brief (June-August) tourist season. February in Finland is not my idea of a good time. During particularly cold winters, Helsinki's bus #19 extends its route over the frozen bay to a suburban island! When summer arrives, the entire population jumps in with street singing and beach-blanket vigor.

Money
There are about 5 Finnish markka (mk) in a U.S. dollar. One markka is about 20 cents.

Language
The Finnish language is a difficult Finno-Ugric language originating east of Russia's Ural Mountains and related in

Europe only to Hungarian. Finland is officially bilingual; 6 percent of the country speaks Swedish as a first language. You'll notice that Helsinki is called Helsingfors in Swedish. Many street signs list places in both languages. Since English is Finland's third language, you'll find that Finns speak less English than their Scandinavian neighbors. Still, nearly every educated young person will speak effortless English. The only essential word needed for a quick visit is *Kiitos* (key toes)—that's "Thank you," and locals love to hear it. "*Kippis*" ("keep peace") is what you say before you down a shot of Finnish vodka or some cloudberry liquer.

And now, on to Helsinki—via a cruise ship.

Sailing from Stockholm to Helsinki

The next best thing to being in Helsinki is getting there. Europe's most enjoyable cruise starts with lovely archipelago scenery, a setting sun, and a royal smorgasbord dinner. Dance till you drop and sauna till you drip. Budget travel rarely feels this hedonistic. Then it's Hello, Helsinki.

Sailing from Stockholm to Helsinki

Planning Your Time

When planning your cruise consider time desired in Helsinki (one day is normally enough) and departure day (Friday and Saturday are more crowded and expensive). Also consider efficient arrangement of schedule ripples caused by the ship. Assuming you take two night boats, and you sleep into and out of Stockholm by train, you'll have 2 days in Stockholm with no nights. Stockholm is worth 2 days on a 3-week Scandinavian trip, but 4 nights in a row in transit is pretty intense. Doable, but intense.

Orientation

Two fine and fiercely competitive lines, Viking and Silja, connect the capitals of Sweden and Finland daily and nightly. The scenic 14-hour cruise passes through 3 hours of the countless islands that buffer Stockholm from the open sea. Each line offers state-of-the-art ships with luxurious smorgasbord meals, reasonable cabins, plenty of entertainment (discos, saunas, gambling), and enough duty-free shopping to sink a ship.

The Cruise Lines: Viking and Silja

The Pepsi and Coke of the Scandinavian cruise industry vie to outdo each other with bigger and fancier boats. The ships are big—56,000 tons, nearly 200 yards long, and with 2,700 beds, the largest (and some of the cheapest) luxury hotels in Scandinavia. Many other lines buy their boats used from Viking and Silja.

Which line is best? You could count showers and compare shoeshines, but basically each line almost goes overboard to win the loyalty of the 9 million duty-free-crazy Swedes and Finns who make the trip each year. Viking, with an older fleet, is about 100 kr per round-trip cheaper. While both lines offer Eurail travelers free passage, Silja requires passengers to rent a bed (about 100 kr each way) and Viking lets stowaways (or those who find the boat booked up) sleep for free on chairs, sofas, and under the stars or stairs. While Silja offers those with a Scanrail pass free crossings to Turku and 50 percent off to Helsinki, Viking gives only a 30 percent discount with these train passes.

Cruise Schedules

Both lines sail daily from Stockholm and Helsinki, usually leaving at 18:00 and arriving the next morning at 8:00 or 9:00. There are morning departures, too, but overnight crossings are more fun and efficient. Both lines also sail daily between Stockholm and Turku, Finland.

Cost

Fares vary with the season and are inconsistent. Check both lines by telephone. Fridays throughout the year and mid-June to mid-August are most expensive (and crowded). Even in high season, a round-trip with the cheapest bed (in a below-sea-level quad) is remarkably cheap: about $100 (700 kr on Viking, 800 kr on Silja). Viking lets vagabonds sail without a bed (500 kr round-trip, deck class, peak season). Off-season is about 200 kr less (round-trip on each line). Beds cost the same throughout the year, starting at around 100 kr (under the car deck, quads) and going up with the elevator. Viking has very simple "Economy Cabins" with 70 kr beds. Each ship offers a whale of a smorgasbord.

The fares are so cheap because the boats operate tax-free and the hordes of locals who sail to shop and drink duty- and tax-free spend a fortune on board. It's a very large operation—mostly for locals. The boats are filled with about 60 percent Finns, 35 percent Swedes, and 5 percent cruisers from other countries. Last year, the average passenger spent nearly as much on booze and duty-free items as he did for the boat fare (about 500 kr).

Reservations

Making reservations is easy by phone in Copenhagen or Stockholm, or even from the U.S.A. If you want a bed and are traveling in summer or on a Friday, make a reservation as soon as you can commit to a date. You can pick up and pay for your reserved ticket at the terminal an hour before sailing. (Viking Line, tel. 08/714 5600 in Stockholm, 33 32 60 36 in Copenhagen; Silja Line tel. 08/22 21 40 in Stockholm, 33 14 40 80 in Copenhagen.) You can also get a ticket through any travel agent in Scandinavia (same price plus their booking fee, if any).

Sleeping Free

While most new boats have no slum beds, there are older boats on the Turku sailings that may have free dorm beds for vagabonds. If you end up on a boat with no cabin (allowed on Viking, necessary if everything's booked up), you can dance, drink, or gamble until the wee hours with the Finns, knowing your bag is locked safely from port to port in the luggage check room.

Time Change

Finland is 1 hour ahead of Sweden. Sailing from Stockholm to Helsinki, operate on Swedish time until you go to bed, then set your watch ahead an hour. Morning schedules are Finnish time (and vice versa when you return).

Meals

The cruise is famous for its smorgasbords, and understandably so. Board the ship hungry. Dinner is self-serve in two sittings, one immediately upon departure, the other 2 hours later. The scenery is worth being on deck for, but if you call in advance you can reserve a window seat. If you board without a reservation, go to the headwaiter and make one. Breakfast buffets are 50 kr, dinner buffets 125 kr. Pick up the "How to Eat a Smorgasbord" brochure. The key is to take small portions and pace yourself. Drinks (25 kr) or free water can be ordered from the waiters. There are also several reasonable or classy a la carte restaurants on board for lighter eaters or those on a budget.

Sauna

Each ship has a sauna. This costs about 45 kr extra. You should reserve a time on boarding. Saunas are half-price or even free in the morning (for those with a cabin towel).

Banking

The change desk on board has bad rates but no fee, which means it's actually a better deal than a Helsinki bank for those changing less than $100. There are about 5 Finnish markka (mk) in a U.S. dollar. Helsinki banks charge 15 mk for cash and 20 mk for traveler's checks, while the change desk in the boat changes cash for no fee and charges 20 mk for checks. For a quick visit to Helsinki, just change some of your Swedish kroner. While city sightseeing tours can be paid for in kroner, you'll need local currency for shops and museums.

Terminal Locations
In Stockholm, Viking is more central (free shuttle service on bus #45 from the Slussen T-bana stop), you'll see the ship parked just past the Gamla Stan. For Silja, take the free and frequent bus from the Ropsten T-bana station or get off the T-bana one stop before at "Gardet" and walk for about 10 minutes to the terminal. In Helsinki, both lines are perfectly central, a 10-minute walk from the market, Senate Square, and shopping district.

Terminal Buildings
These are well organized and functional, with facilities such as cafés, lockers, tourist information desks, lounges, and phones. Remember, 2,000 passengers come and go with each boat. Customs is a snap. I've never shown my passport. Boats open 1 hour before departure.

Parking
Both lines offer safe and handy 50 kr/day parking in Stockholm. Viking's ticket machine takes 5- and 10-kr coins (come with 90 kr for 46 hrs). Keep inserting money until you see the date and time of your return on the meter, then hit the red button and leave the ticket on your dashboard. Park your car here on arrival in Stockholm, and leave it while you sightsee Stockholm, take the cruise, and tour Helsinki.

Open Jaws
Consider an "open jaws" plan, sailing from Stockholm into Helsinki and returning to Stockholm from Turku. The cheaper round-trip boat fare saves enough to pay for the 2-hour train ride from Helsinki to Turku. The Turku boats have free couchettes in the bilge, but the boats are smaller and lack the cruise ship excitement. Passengers are rushed on and off since the boat doesn't stay long in the port.

Day Privileges
If you're spending two nights in a row on the Stockholm-Helsinki boat, you have access to your stateroom all day

long. If you like, you can sleep in and linger over breakfast, long after the boat has docked. But there's really way too much to do in Helsinki to take advantage of these privileges (unless you take the round-trip passage twice, on four successive nights—a reasonable option given the high cost of hotels and meals on shore and the frustration of trying to see Helsinki in a day).

Staying Overnight in Helsinki
If you're staying in Helsinki, your boat line can get you a $100 double in a $200 hotel, but you can find a cheaper room by telephoning my budget listings.

Helsinki
Helsinki feels close to Russia. It is. Much of it reminds me of St. Petersburg. It's no wonder Hollywood chose to film *Dr. Zhivago*, *Reds*, and *Gorky Park* here. (They filmed the Moscow Railway Station scenes in *Dr. Zhivago* in the low red-brick building near the Viking Terminal.) There is a huge and impressive Russian Orthodox church overlooking the harbor, a large Russian community, and several fine Russian restaurants.

In the early 1800s, when the Russians took Finland from Sweden, they moved the capital eastward from Turku, making Helsinki the capital of their "autonomous duchy." I asked a woman in the tourist office if a particular café was made for Russian officers. In a rare spasm of candor (this was during the Cold War), she said, "All of 19th-century Helsinki was made for Russian officers."

Today Helsinki is gray and green. A little windy and cold, it looks like it's stuck somewhere in the north near the Russian border. But it makes the best of its difficult situation and will leave you impressed and glad to have dropped in. Start with the 2-hour Hello Helsinki bus tour that meets the boat at the dock. Enjoy Helsinki's ruddy harborfront market, count goosebumps in her churches, and dive into Finnish culture in the open-air folk museum.

Europe's most neoclassical city has many architectural overleafs, and it tends to turn guests into fans of town planning and architecture. Its buildings, designs, fashions, and people fit sensitively into their surroundings. Dissimilar elements are fused into a complex but comfortable whole. It's a very intimate and human place.

Planning Your Time

On a 3-week trip through Scandinavia, Helsinki is worth the time between two successive nights on the cruise ship—about 9 hours. Take the orientation bus tour upon arrival, mingle through the market, buy and eat a picnic, and drop by the TI. People-watch and browse through downtown to the National Museum. For the afternoon, choose between the National Museum, the Open-Air Folk Museum, the 15:30 English walking tour (from the TI, if scheduled), or a harbor boat tour. Enjoy a cup of coffee in the Cafe Kappeli before boarding time. Sail away while eating another smorgasbord dinner.

Orientation

(tel. code to Helsinki from outside Finland: 358-0)
Helsinki is a colorful shopping town of 500,000 people. The compact city center is a great area to roam; great for a brisk walk.

Tourist Information

Helsinki has tourist information offices at the boat terminals, inside the train station, and (closest to the ferries) on the market square (market square office open 8:30-18:00, Saturday 8:30-13:00, closed Sunday, shorter hours off-season, tel. 1693 757 or 174 088, fax 169 3839). They are uniformly friendly, helpful, well stocked in brochures, and blond(e). Pick up the city map, the "Route Map" (public transit), "Helsinki on Foot" (six well-described and mapped walking tours), and the monthly *Helsinki This Week* magazine which lists sights, hours, and events. Ask about the 3T tourist tram and the city walking tours (2/week, 30 mk). Go over your sightseeing plans. You can call 058 for recorded events and sights hours (in English) any time.

Transportation

Train info, tel. 101 01 15. Ferry info: Viking Line, tel. 12351; Silja Line, tel. 180 4455. Remember, Finland is one hour ahead of Sweden. If you're returning to Stockholm, the boat departs Helsinki at Finnish time. Helsinki's area code is 90 and Finland's country code is 358. When calling Helsinki from outside of Finland, add the country code and drop the 9 (358-0-local number).

Getting Around

With the public transit route map and a little mental elbow grease, the buses and trams are easy, giving you the city by the tail. Tickets (9 mk) are good for an hour of travel, and are purchased from the driver. The Helsinki Card (105 mk) gives you free entry to city sights and use of all buses and trams for 24 hours. The tourist tram, 3T, makes the rounds of most of the towns major sights, letting you stop and go for 9 mk an hour. The TI has a helpful explanatory brochure (not available on the bus).

Sights—Helsinki

▲▲▲The Downtown Helsinki Walk from the Harbor to Train Station—The colorful produce market on the market square thrives daily 7:00-14:00 and 15:30-20:00 (closed Saturday afternoon and Sunday). At the head of the harbor, facing the cruise ships, this is Helsinki's center. Don't miss the busy two-tone red-brick indoor market hall adjacent. Across the street you'll see the City Tourist Office. Drop in to ask questions and check out the huge aerial photo of downtown. The round door next to the TI leads into the delightful Jugendsalen. Designed, apparently, by a guy named Art Nouveau, this free and pleasant information center for locals offers interesting historical exhibits and a public WC. The art deco interior is a knockout (Monday-Friday 9:00-18:00, Sunday 12:00-18:00, closed Saturday, Pohjoisesplanadi 19).

One block inland behind the Tourist Office are the fine neoclassical Senate Square and the Lutheran Cathedral. You'll pass the Schroder Sport Shop on Unioninkatu with a great selection of popular Finnish-made Rapula fishing lures—ideal for the fisherman on your gift list.

Across the street from the TI, in the park facing the square, is my favorite café in northern Europe, the Cafe Kappeli. When you've got some time, dip into this turn-

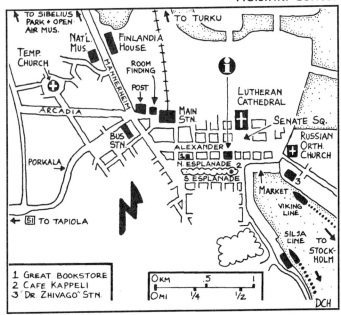

Helsinki Center

1 Great Bookstore
2 Cafe Kappeli
3 "Dr. Zhivago" Stn.

of-the-century gazebo-like oasis of coffee, pastry, and relax-
ation. Built in the 19th century, it was a popular hangout for
local intellectuals and artists. Today the café closest to the
market offers the romantic tourist waiting for his ship to sail
a great 8 mk cup of coffee memory (unguarded WC just
inside the door).

Behind the café runs the entertaining park, sandwiched
between the north and south Esplanadi—Helsinki's top
shopping boulevard. Walk it. The north (tourist office) side
is interesting for window shopping, people-watching, and
sun-worshiping. You'll pass several stores and the huge
Academic Bookstore, designed by Alvar Aalto (nearby at 1
Keskuskatu), which has a great map and travel guide section.
Finally you'll come to the prestigious Stockman's department store—Finland's Harrod's. This best, oldest, and most
expensive store in town has fine displays of local design. Just
beyond is the main intersection in town, Esplanadi and
Mannerheimintie. Nearby you'll see the famous *Three Smiths*
statue. (Locals say, "If a virgin walks by, they'll strike the
anvil." It doesn't work. I tried.)

A block to the right, through a busy shopping center, is the harsh (in a serene way) architecture of the central train station, designed by Saarinen in 1916. The four people on the facade symbolize the peasant farmers with lamps coming into the Finnish capital. Wander around inside. Continuing past the Posti and the statue, return to Mannerheimintie, which leads to the large white Finlandia Hall, another Aalto masterpiece. While it's not normally open, there are often two tours a day in the summer (ask at the TI). Across the street is the excellent little Finnish National Museum (looks like a church, designed by Finland's first three great architects), and a few blocks behind that is the sit-down-and-wipe-a-tear beautiful rock church, Temppeliaukio. Sit. Enjoy the music. It's a wonderful place to end this Welcome to Helsinki walk.

From nearby Arkadiankatu Street, bus #24 will take you to the Sibelius monument in a lovely park. The same ticket is good on a later #24. Ride to the end of the line—the bridge to the Seurasaari island and Finland's open-air folk museum. From here, bus #24 returns to the Esplanadi.

▲▲▲**Orientation Bus Tour**—A fast, very good 2-hour introductory tour leaves daily from both terminals immediately after the ships dock (unless there are two arrivals, in which case some travelers will have an hour to walk down and see the market in action). The rapid-fire two- or three-language tour costs 85 mk (120 Swedish kroner) and gives a good historic overview—a look at all the important buildings from the Olympic Stadium to embassy row, with too-fast 10-minute stops at the Lutheran Cathedral, the Sibelius monument, and the Church in the Rock (Temppeliaukio). You'll learn strange facts, such as how they took down the highest steeple in town during World War II so the Soviet bombers flying in from Estonia, just 55 miles over the water, couldn't see their target.

If you're on a tight budget and don't care to get the general overview of Helsinki, you can do the essence of this tour on your own as explained in my city walk (above). But I thoroughly enjoyed listening to the guide. He sounded like an audio shredder that was occasionally turned off so English could come out. The tour drops you off at the market square, near the national museum (if you ask), or at your hotel by 11:30.

If you'd like more time in the Church of the Rock, leave the tour there and consider walking 3 blocks to the National Museum and the Finlandia Hall. Architects will prefer the 2½ hour, 95 mk tours, which leave from the Silja terminal at 10:00 and 11:00, which are basically the same, with a trip through the Aalto-designed Technical University at Otamieni and out to the planned "garden city" suburb of Tapiola. There is a shorter (no stop at Lutheran Cathedral), cheaper tour that's nearly as good (60 mk and included on the Helsinki Card, daily in summer at 11:00 and 13:00, from the train station, tel. 5885 166), but I like the "pick you up at the boat and drop you at your hotel or back on the market square" efficiency of the 9:30 tour. Buy your ticket on board or at the tourist desk in the terminal (availability no problem).

▲▲**Lutheran Cathedral**—With its prominent green dome overlooking the city and harbor, this church is the masterpiece of Carl Ludwig Engel. Open the pew gate and sit to savor neoclassical Nirvana. Finished in 1852, the interior is pure architectural truth. (Open 9:00-19:00, Saturday and Sunday 9:00-18:00, winter until 17:00.) From the top of the steps, study Europe's finest neoclassical square. The Senate building is on your left. The small blue stone building with the slanted mansard roof in the far left corner is from 1757, one of just two pre-Russian conquest buildings remaining in Helsinki. On the right is the University building. Czar Alexander II, a friend of Finland's, is honored by the statue in the square. The huge staircase leading up to the cathedral is a popular meeting and tanning point in Helsinki.

▲▲▲**Temppeliaukio Church**—Another great piece of church architecture, this was blasted out of solid rock and capped with a copper and skylight dome. It's normally filled with live or recorded music and awestruck visitors. I almost cried. Another form of simple truth, it's impossible to describe. Grab a pew. Gawk upward at a 14-mile-long coil of copper wire. Look at the bull's-eye and ponder God. Forget your camera. Just sit in the middle, ignore the crowds, and be thankful for peace—under your feet is an air raid shelter that can accommodate 6,000 people. (Open Monday-Saturday 10:00-20:00, Sunday 12:00-14:00, 15:20-15:45, and 17:00-18:00.) To experience the church in action, attend the Lutheran English service (Sunday at 14:00, tel.

406091) or one of the many concerts. You can buy individual slides or the picture book.

▲**Sibelius Monument**—Six-hundred stainless steel pipes shimmer over a rock in a park to honor Finland's greatest composer. Notice the face of Sibelius (which the artist was forced to add to silence the critics of his abstract work). Bus #24 stops here (or catch a quick glimpse on the left from the bus) on its way to the Open-Air Folk Museum. The 3T tram, which runs more frequently, stops a few blocks away.

▲**Seurasaari Open-Air Folk Museum**—Inspired by Stockholm's Skansen, also on a lovely island on the edge of town, this is a collection of 100 historic buildings gathered from every corner of Finland. Many of the buildings are staffed with an information person 11:00-17:00. It's wonderfully furnished and gives rushed visitors a great opportunity to sample the far reaches of Finland without leaving the capital city. Buy the 10 mk guidebook.

Off-season it's quiet, just you, log cabins, and birch trees—almost not worth a look. (The park is free, 10 mk to enter the buildings, daily June-August 11:00-17:00; May and September Monday-Friday 9:00-15:00, Saturday and Sunday 11:00-17:00). In winter, the park is open but the buildings are closed. Ride bus #24 to the end of the line and walk across the quaint footbridge. Call or check at the TI for English tour (usually at 11:30 and 15:30) and evening folk dance schedules (usually Tuesday, Thursday, and Sunday at 19:00, tel. 484562).

For a 10 mk bottomless cup of coffee in a cozy-like-someone's-home setting, stop by the café near the Seurasaari bridge, up the road at Tamminiementie 1 (June-August 11:00-23:00). Great bagels—and Chopin, too.

▲▲**National Museum**—This is a pleasant, easy-to-handle collection (covering Finland's story from A to Z with good English descriptions) in a grand building designed by three of Finland's greatest early architects. While the neoclassical furniture, portraits of Russia's last czars around an impressive throne, and the folk costumes are interesting, the highlight is the Finno-Ugric exhibit downstairs, with a 20-page English guide to help explain the Finns, Estonians, Lapps, Hungarians, and their more obscure Finno-Ugric cousins (10 mk, daily 11:00-16:00, Tuesday 18:00-21:00, across the street from the Finlandia Hall, tel. 40501). The museum café has light meals and Finnish treats such as lingonberry juice and reindeer quiche.

Finlandia Hall—Alvar Aalto's most famous building in his native Finnland means little to the non-architect without a tour (15 mk, in summer, noon and 14:00, tel. 40241).

▲▲Uspensky Russian Orthodox Cathedral—Hovering above the market square, blessing the harbor, and facing the Lutheran Cathedral as Russian culture faces Europe's, is a fine icon experience and western Europe's largest Russian Orthodox church (Tuesday-Friday 9:30-16:00, Saturday 9:00-12:00, Sunday 12:00-15:00).

▲Harbor tours—Several boat companies line the market square offering 90-minute, 50 mk cruises around the waterfront nearly every hour 10:00-17:30. The narration is slow-moving and in three languages, but if the weather's good and you're looking for something one step above a snooze in the park, it's a nice break.

▲Flea Market—Lately, Hietalahti Market, Finland's biggest flea market, is particularly interesting, with the many Russian and Baltic people hawking whatever they can for a little hard currency (Monday-Saturday 8:00-14:00, summer evenings Monday-Friday 15:00-21:00). If you brake for garage sales, it's well worth the 15-minute walk from the harbor.

Suomenlinna—The "fortified island" is a 20-minute ferry or water bus ride (15 mk-20 mk round-trip, on the half hour) from the market square. The old fort is now a popular park with several museums.

Sauna—Finland's vaporized fountain of youth is the sauna. Public saunas are a dying breed these days, since saunas are standard equipment in nearly every Finnish apartment and home. Your boat or hotel has a sauna. Your youth hostel probably even has one. For a real experience, ask about the Finnish Sauna Society (70 mk, bus #20 for 20 minutes in a park on the waterfront, men-only most nights, Thursday is women's night). For a cheap and easy public sauna, go to the Olympic swimming pool at the Olympic stadium (10 mk, pool and sauna open 7:00-20:00).

Nightlife—Remember that Finland was the first country to give women the vote. The sexes are equal in the bars and on the dance floor. Finns are easily approachable and tourists are not a headache to the locals (as they are in places like Paris and Munich). While it's easy to make friends, anything alcoholic is very expensive. For the latest on hot night spots, read the English insert of the *City* magazine that lists the "Best" of everything in Helsinki. For very cheap fun, Hietaranta beach is where the local kids hang out (and even skinny-dip) at 22:00 or 23:00. This city is one of Europe's safest after dark.

Sleeping in Helsinki
(5mk = about $1, tel. code from outside of Finland: 358-0)

Standard budget hotel doubles start at $100. But there are many special deals, and dorm and hostel alternatives. You have four basic budget options—cheap youth hostels, student dorms turned "summer hotels," plain and basic low-class hotels, or expensive business-class hotels at a special summer or weekend clearance sale rate.

Sleep code: **S**=Single, **D**=Double/Twin, **T**=Triple, **Q**=Quad, **B**=Bath/Shower, **WC**=Toilet, **CC**=Credit Card (**V**isa, **M**astercard, **A**mex).

Summer (mid-June-mid-August) is "off-season" in Helsinki, as are Friday, Saturday, and Sunday nights the rest of the year. You can arrive in the morning and expect to find a budget room. In the train station next to Track 4 (a pleasant 20-minute walk from your boat, or tram 3B from Silja, bus #13 from Viking, on arrival only) is the **Hotellikeskus** room-finding service (June-August 9:00-19:00, Sunday 10:00-18:00; off-season 10:00-17:00 Monday-Friday only). For 12 mk (hotels) or 5 mk (hostels), they'll book you a bed in the price range of your choice. They know what wild bargains are available. Consider a luxury hotel clearance deal, which may cost $20 more than the cheapies. Ask about any Helsinki card "specials," which lower prices mid-June–early September and on weekends. Their 12 mk fee is reasonable, but they're happy to do the job over the phone for free. Call from the harbor or Stockholm (tel. 90/171133).

Sleeping in Hostels

Eurohostel is a modern hostel located a block from the Viking terminal or a 10-minute walk from the market square

(S-160 mk, D-220 mk, T-330 mk, including sheets, private lockable closets, and morning sauna, less 15 mk per person with hostel cards, breakfast 25 kr, doubles and triples can be shared with a stranger of the same sex for 110 mk per bed; Linnankatu 9, 00160 Helsinki, tel. 90/664452, fax 655044). It's packed with facilities including a TV room, laundry room, a members' kitchen with a refrigerator that lets you lock up your caviar and beer, a cheap cafeteria, and plenty of good budget information on travel to Russia or the Baltics. (Eurohostel sells *Rick Steves' Best of the Baltics and Russia*, the guidebook that I co-wrote with Ian Watson.)

Kallio Retkeilymaja is cozy, cheery, central, well run, and very cheap (small—only 30 beds; 50 mk for dorm bed for boys, or a bed in 5-bed rooms for girls, including sheets and a locker, kitchen facilities, closed 10:30-15:00, open June-August; Porthaniankatu 2, tel. 90/70992590). From Market Square, take the metro or tram 3T, #1 or #2 to Hakaniemi Square Market.

Olympic Stadium Hostel (Stadionin Retkeilymaja, IYHF). This is big, crowded, impersonal, and a last-resort bed. (50 mk per bed in 8- to 12-bed rooms, 70 mk per bed in doubles, sheets for 15 mk, 15 mk extra with no youth hostel card; open all year, closed daily 10:00-16:00 off-season, tel. 496071.) Take tram 7A to the Olympic Stadium.

Sleeping in Classy "Real" Hotels

Hotel Anna is plush and very central (near Mannerheimintie and Esplanadi, a 15-minute walk from the boat). It is one of the best values in town (D-400 mk in summer with breakfast and private showers, 1 Annankatu, tel. 648011, fax 602 664). **Hotel Olympia** is often about the least expensive hotel in town (D-320 mk in summer with private showers and breakfast; not so central but on the 3B or #1 tram line at the Sport Hall stop, 2 Lantinen Brahenkatu, tel. 750801, fax 750 801). Both of these places charge 600 mk during business season.

Sleeping in Dreary, Old World Inns

Matkakoti Erottajanpuisto is a more traditional old inn (D-230 mk, T-300 mk, Q-330 mk, 20 mk less per room in summer, shower down the hall, no breakfast room but 25 mk for it in bed; a 10-minute walk from the market square, jog left at the end of Esplanadi, Uudenmaankatu 9, tel. 90/642 169, fax 680 2757) with a fine living room, but only one shower for 15 rooms.

Matkustajakoti Lonnrot is a friendly but borderline dreary place in a very central location (D-220 mk, 280 mk in business season; shower down the hall, breakfast in the room, the "best room" is given out for the same cheap price upon request; continue straight at the top of North Esplanadi, Lonnrotinkatu 16, tel. 90/693 2590, fax 693 2482).

Eating in Helsinki

In Helsinki, Russian food is an interesting option. Most popular, with meals for around 100 mk, are the **Troikka** (good Russian food in a tsarific setting, Caloniukesenkatu 3, tel. 445229 for reservations), and **Kasakka** (old Russian style, Meritullinkatu 13, tel. 1356-288). Seafood is another local specialty. Many restaurants serve daily lunch specials for around 40 mk.

The **Palace Café**, overlooking the harbor and market square above the Palace Hotel, is a good, not-too-exorbitant place for lunch. The Lutheran Cathedral, National Museum, and Academic bookstore all have handy cafés. For a meal with folk music, ask at the tourist office about the dinner show at the **Seurasaari Open-Air Folk Museum**.

The best food values are, of course, the department store cafeterias and a picnic assembled from the colorful stalls on the harbor and nearby bakery. Take advantage of the red-brick indoor market on the edge of the square. At the harbor you'll also find several local fast-food stalls and delicious fresh fish (cooked if you like), explosive little red berries, and sweet carrots. While the open-air market is the most fun, produce is cheaper in large grocery stores. Each open-air market has a popular-with-local-shoppers "tent café."

In the train station, the **Eliel self-service** restaurant offers reasonable midday specials in a spendid architectural setting.

Transportation Connections

Helsinki and Stockholm: The Silja and Viking lines sail between Helsinki and Stockholm daily/nightly. (See the beginning of this chapter for details.)

Helsinki and Tallinn, Estonia: There are several crossings daily between Helsinki and Tallinn. One-way fares for regular ferries cost $20 (4-hr trip) and the hydrofoil costs $45 (2-hr trip). Estonian New Line (tel. 358/0/680-2499 in Helsinki) has the most frequent departures. The best local information source is the Eurohostel (358/0/664452).

Near Helsinki: Turku and Naantali

Turku and Naantali get good publicity, but I found these towns a little disappointing. The train ride is nothing special, Turku is a pale shadow of Helsinki, and Naantali is cute, commercial, and offers little (if you've seen or will see Sigtuna, near Stockholm).

Turku, the historic, old capital of Finland, is just a 2-hour train ride from Helsinki (6/day, 70 mk, free with Eurail or save 50% by getting RR connection with an "open-jaws" boat ticket). Turku has a handicraft museum in a cluster of wooden houses (the only part of town that survived a devastating fire in the early 1800s), an impressive old cathedral, and a busy market square. Viking and Silja boats sail each evening from Turku to Stockholm at 21:30 (the fare from here to Stockholm saves you enough to pay for the train ride from Helsinki to Turku).

Naantali, a well-preserved medieval town with a quaint harbor, is an easy bus ride (30 min, 12 mk, 4/hr) from Turku.

APPENDIX

Public Transportation

You can tour Scandinavia efficiently and enjoyably by train and bus. You even have a few options that drivers don't. If you sleep on the very comfortable Nordic trains, destinations not worth driving to on a short trip become feasible. Add your own Scandinavian highlights. Consider a swing through Finland's eastern lakes district or the scenic ride to Trondheim. I'd go overnight whenever possible on any ride 6 or more hours long.

Scandinavia: Main Train Lines

My chapter on Norway is heavy on fjord scenery (my kind of problem). Fjord country buses, boats, and trains connect, but not without lengthy 1- to 3-hour layovers. "Norway in a Nutshell" is an exception. The Flam-Bergen boat is a great fjord finale.

Train, Bus, and Boat Connections

Pick up exact schedules as you travel, available free at any tourist office. Some lines make fewer runs or even close in the off-season.

A trip linking all of my recommended destinations easily justifies the purchase of a 21-day Nordtourist pass ($400 first class, $300 second class, about $300 and $200, first and second class for those under 26, buy at any Scandinavian station, be careful not to purchase a Scandia-rail pass in the U.S.A. which is more expensive than a Nordtourist pass) or a 21-day Eurailpass ($598, first class only, from travel agents in the U.S. only). The Eurailpass covers all the train rides listed, the boats from Stockholm to Helsinki and Turku, the Denmark-Sweden ferry, and the Halsskov-Knudshoved ride. The Nordtourist pass is good on all of these (except the Stockholm-Helsinki ride, only 50%), all Danish state ferries, and the Kristiansand-Hirtshals trip. Your travel agent has brochures and more information.

	Departures per Day	Hours
Copenhagen to:		
Hillerod (Frederiksborg)	40	½
Louisiana (Helsinger train to Humlebaek)	40	½
Roskilde	16	½
Odense (tel. 33 14 88 80)	16	½
Helsingor (ferry to Sweden)	40	½
Stockholm	6-8	8
Vaxjo via Alvesta	6	5
Oslo	4	10
Berlin via Gedser	2	9
Amsterdam	2	11
Frankfurt/Rhine castles	4	10
Stockholm to:		
Kalmar	6	8
	(1 night train)	
Helsinki	2	14

Stockholm to:	Departures per Day	Hours
Turku	2	10
Uppsala	30	1
Oslo	3	7
Vaxjo to glassworks	TI tour or side trip by bus	
Vaxjo to Kalmar	9	1½
Helsinki to Turku	7	2½

Oslo to:

Lillehammer	12	2½
Andalsnes	3	6½
Bergen	4	7-8
Trondheim	3	7-8

Norway's Mountain and Fjord Country
Lillehammer to:

Andalsnes	4	4
Lom (change at Otta)	3	4
Andalsnes to Alesund by bus (with each arriving train)	2	½
Andalsnes over Trollstigvege to Geiranger Fjord	early each morning	4
Lom to Sogndal	2	4
(bus departures 8:50 and 15:50, summer only)		

Bergen to:
Haukelegrend, one trip possible daily, several changes

Alesund	1	10

South Norway
Setesdal Valley, Hovden to:

Kristiansand	2	5

Kristiansand to:

Oslo	6	4-5
Hirtshals, Denmark by ferry	4	4

Denmark
Departure from:

Hirtshals to Arhus	16	2½
Arhus to Odense	16	2
Odense to Svendborg	16	1
Svendborg to Aero, ferry	5 (summer)	1
Aero to Kobenhavn	5	5
Halsskov-Knudshoved	26	1

Telephones

Too many timid tourists never figure out the phones. They work, and are essential to smart travel. Public phone booths are much cheaper than using the more convenient hotel phones. While each country now has telephone cards, there are plenty of booths that still accept coins. If you'll be in a country for a while and plan to make a lot of calls, pick up a telephone card at a post office or newstand. A telephone will not give change for a coin. Push the carry-forward button and you can make another call.

Incidentally, using directory assistance in Scandinavia costs about the same as telephone sex. Really.

Country	AT&T	MCI	SPRINT
Denmark	800 100 10	800 100 22	800 108 77
Sweden	020 795 611	020 795 922	020 799 011
Norway	050 120 11	050 129 12	050 128 77

Tourist Information

In the U.S.A., write to Norway, Sweden, Denmark, and Finland c/o Scandinavian Tourist Board, 655 3rd Ave., New York, NY 10017, or call 212/949-2333.

INDEX

RICK STEVES'

FREE TRAVEL NEWSLETTER/CATALOG

My Europe Through the Back Door travel company will help you travel better *because* you're on a budget — not in spite of it. Call us at (206) 771-8303, and we'll send you our *free newsletter/catalog* packed full of info on budget travel, railpasses, guidebooks, videos, travel bags and tours:

EUROPEAN RAILPASSES

We sell the full range of European railpasses, and with every Eurailpass we give you these important extras — *free:* my hour-long "How to get the most out of your railpass" video; your choice of one of my ten "Best of..." regional guidebooks and phrasebooks; and our sage advice on your 1-page itinerary. Call us for a free copy of our 64-page *1995 Back Door Guide to European Railpasses.*

BACK DOOR TOURS

We offer a variety of European tours for those who want to travel in the Back Door style, but without the transportation and hotel hassles. If a tour with a small group, modest Back Door accomodations, lots of physical exercise, and no tips or hidden charges sounds like your idea of fun, call us for details.

CONVERTIBLE BACK DOOR BAG $75

At 9"x21"x13" our specially designed, sturdy bag is maximum carry-on-the-plane size (fits under the seat) and your key to footloose and fancy-free travel. Made of rugged water resistant cordura nylon, it converts easily from a smart looking suitcase to a handy rucksack. It has padded hide-away shoulder straps, top and side handles, and a detachable shoulder strap (for use as a suitcase). Lockable perimeter zippers allow easy access to the roomy 2,500 cubic inch central compartment. Two large outside compartments are perfect for frequently used items. We'll even toss in a nylon stuff bag. More than 40,000 Back Door travelers have used these bags around the world. I live out of one for three months at a time. Available in black, grey, navy blue and teal green.

MONEYBELT $8

Absolutely required for European travel, our sturdy nylon, ultra-light, under-the-pants pouch is just big enough to carry your essentials (passport, airline tickets, travelers checks, gummi bears, and so on) comfortably. I won't travel without one, and neither should you. Comes in neutral beige, with a nylon zipper. One size fits all.

All items are field tested by Rick Steves and completely guaranteed.
Prices are good through 1995 (maybe longer), and include shipping (allow 2 to 3 weeks).
WA residents add 8.2% tax. Sorry, no credit cards or phone orders. Send checks in US $ to:

Europe Through the Back Door ❖ 120 Fourth Avenue North
PO Box 2009, Edmonds, WA 98020 ❖ Phone: (206)771-8303

Other Books from John Muir Publications

Travel Books by Rick Steves
Asia Through the Back Door, 4th ed., 400 pp. $16.95

Europe 101: History, Art, and Culture for the Traveler, 4th ed., 372 pp. $15.95

Mona Winks: Self-Guided Tours of Europe's Top Museums, 2nd ed., 456 pp. $16.95

Rick Steves' Best of the Baltics and Russia, 1995 ed. 144 pp. $9.95

Rick Steves' Best of Europe, 1995 ed., 544 pp. $16.95

Rick Steves' Best of France, Belgium, and the Netherlands, 1995 ed., 240 pp. $12.95

Rick Steves' Best of Germany, Austria, and Switzerland, 1995 ed., 240 pp. $12.95

Rick Steves' Best of Great Britain, 1995 ed., 192 pp. $11.95

Rick Steves' Best of Italy, 1995 ed., 208 pp. $11.95

Rick Steves' Best of Scandinavia, 1995 ed., 192 pp. $11.95

Rick Steves' Best of Spain and Portugal, 1995 ed., 192 pp. $11.95

Rick Steves' Europe Through the Back Door, 13th ed., 480 pp. $17.95

Rick Steves' French Phrase Book, 2nd ed., 112 pp. $4.95

Rick Steves' German Phrase Book, 2nd ed., 112 pp. $4.95

Rick Steves' Italian Phrase Book, 2nd ed., 112 pp. $4.95

Rick Steves' Spanish and Portuguese Phrase Book, 2nd ed., 288 pp. $5.95

Rick Steves' French/German/Italian Phrase Book, 288 pp. $6.95

A Natural Destination Series
Belize: A Natural Destination, 2nd ed., 304 pp. $16.95

Costa Rica: A Natural Destination, 3rd ed., 400 pp. $17.95

Guatemala: A Natural Destination, 336 pp. $16.95

Undiscovered Islands Series
Undiscovered Islands of the Caribbean, 3rd ed., 264 pp. $14.95

Undiscovered Islands of the Mediterranean, 2nd ed., 256 pp. $13.95

Undiscovered Islands of the U.S. and Canadian West Coast, 288 pp. $12.95

For Birding Enthusiasts
The Birder's Guide to Bed and Breakfasts: U.S. and Canada, 288 pp. $15.95

The Visitor's Guide to the Birds of the Central National Parks: U.S. and Canada, 400 pp. $15.95

The Visitor's Guide to the Birds of the Eastern National Parks: U.S. and Canada, 400 pp. $15.95

The Visitor's Guide to the Birds of the Rocky Mountain National Parks: U.S. and Canada, 432 pp. $15.95

Unique Travel Series
Each is 112 pages and $10.95 paperback.

Unique Arizona
Unique California
Unique Colorado
Unique Florida
Unique New England
Unique New Mexico
Unique Texas
Unique Washington

2 to 22 Days Itinerary Planners
2 to 22 Days in the American Southwest, 1995 ed., 192 pp. $11.95

2 to 22 Days in Asia, 192 pp.
$10.95
2 to 22 Days in Australia,
192 pp. $10.95
2 to 22 Days in California,
1995 ed., 192 pp. $11.95
2 to 22 Days in Eastern
Canada, 1995 ed., 240 pp
$11.95
2 to 22 Days in Florida, 1995
ed., 192 pp. $11.95
2 to 22 Days Around the
Great Lakes, 1995 ed., 192
pp. $11.95
2 to 22 Days in Hawaii, 1995
ed., 192 pp. $11.95
2 to 22 Days in New
England, 1995 ed., 192 pp.
$11.95
2 to 22 Days in New
Zealand, 192 pp. $10.95
2 to 22 Days in the Pacific
Northwest, 1995 ed., 192
pp. $11.95
2 to 22 Days in the Rockies,
1995 ed., 192 pp. $11.95
2 to 22 Days in Texas, 1995
ed., 192 pp. $11.95
2 to 22 Days in Thailand, 192
pp. $10.95
22 Days Around the World,
264 pp. $13.95

Other Terrific Travel Titles
The 100 Best Small Art
Towns in America, 224 pp.
$12.95
Elderhostels: The Students'
Choice, 2nd ed., 304 pp.
$15.95
Environmental Vacations:
Volunteer Projects to Save
the Planet, 2nd ed., 248 pp.
$16.95
A Foreign Visitor's Guide to
America, 224 pp. $12.95
Great Cities of Eastern
Europe, 256 pp. $16.95
Indian America: A Traveler's
Companion, 3rd ed., 432
pp. $18.95
Interior Furnishings
Southwest, 256 pp. $19.95
Opera! The Guide to
Western Europe's Great
Houses, 296 pp. $18.95
Paintbrushes and Pistols:

How the Taos Artists Sold
the West, 288 pp. $17.95
The People's Guide to
Mexico, 9th ed., 608 pp.
$18.95
Ranch Vacations: The
Complete Guide to Guest
and Resort, Fly-Fishing,
and Cross-Country Skiing
Ranches, 3rd ed., 512 pp.
$19.95
The Shopper's Guide to Art
and Crafts in the Hawaiian
Islands, 272 pp. $13.95
The Shopper's Guide to
Mexico, 224 pp. $9.95
Understanding Europeans,
272 pp. $14.95
A Viewer's Guide to Art: A
Glossary of Gods, People,
and Creatures, 144 pp.
$10.95
Watch It Made in the U.S.A.:
A Visitor's Guide to the
Companies that Make Your
Favorite Products, 272 pp.
$16.95

Parenting Titles
Being a Father: Family,
Work, and Self, 176 pp.
$12.95
Preconception: A Woman's
Guide to Preparing for
Pregnancy and
Parenthood, 232 pp. $14.95
Schooling at Home: Parents,
Kids, and Learning, 264
pp., $14.95
Teens: A Fresh Look, 240
pp. $14.95

Automotive Titles
The Greaseless Guide to
Car Care Confidence, 224
pp. $14.95
How to Keep Your
Datsun/Nissan Alive, 544
pp. $21.95
How to Keep Your Subaru
Alive, 480 pp. $21.95
How to Keep Your Toyota
Pickup Alive, 392 pp.
$21.95
How to Keep Your VW Alive,
25th Anniversary ed., 464
pp. spiral bound $25

TITLES FOR YOUNG READERS AGES 8 AND UP

American Origins Series
Each is 48 pages and $12.95 hardcover.
Tracing Our English Roots
Tracing Our French Roots
Tracing Our German Roots
Tracing Our Irish Roots
Tracing Our Italian Roots
Tracing Our Japanese Roots
Tracing Our Jewish Roots
Tracing Our Polish Roots

Bizarre & Beautiful Series
Each is 48 pages, $9.95 paperback, and $14.95 hardcover.
Bizarre & Beautiful Ears
Bizarre & Beautiful Eyes
Bizarre & Beautiful Feelers
Bizarre & Beautiful Noses
Bizarre & Beautiful Tongues

Environmental Titles
Habitats: Where the Wild Things Live, 48 pp. $9.95
The Indian Way: Learning to Communicate with Mother Earth, 114 pp. $9.95
Rads, Ergs, and Cheeseburgers: The Kids' Guide to Energy and the Environment, 108 pp. $13.95
The Kids' Environment Book: What's Awry and Why, 192 pp. $13.95

Extremely Weird Series
Each is 48 pages, $9.95 paperback, and $14.95 hardcover.
Extremely Weird Bats
Extremely Weird Birds
Extremely Weird Endangered Species
Extremely Weird Fishes
Extremely Weird Frogs
Extremely Weird Insects
Extremely Weird Mammals
Extremely Weird Micro Monsters
Extremely Weird Primates
Extremely Weird Reptiles
Extremely Weird Sea Creatures
Extremely Weird Snakes
Extremely Weird Spiders

Kidding Around Travel Series
All are 64 pages and $9.95 paperback, except for *Kidding Around Spain* and *Kidding Around the National Parks of the Southwest*, which are 108 pages and $12.95 paperback.
Kidding Around Atlanta
Kidding Around Boston, 2nd ed.
Kidding Around Chicago, 2nd ed.
Kidding Around the Hawaiian Islands
Kidding Around London
Kidding Around Los Angeles
Kidding Around the National Parks of the Southwest
Kidding Around New York City, 2nd ed.
Kidding Around Paris
Kidding Around Philadelphia
Kidding Around San Diego
Kidding Around San Francisco
Kidding Around Santa Fe
Kidding Around Seattle
Kidding Around Spain
Kidding Around Washington, D.C., 2nd ed.

Kids Explore Series
Written by kids for kids, all are $9.95 paperback.
Kids Explore America's African American Heritage, 128 pp.
Kids Explore the Gifts of Children with Special Needs, 128 pp.
Kids Explore America's Hispanic Heritage, 112 pp.
Kids Explore America's Japanese American Heritage, 144 pp.

Masters of Motion Series
Each is 48 pages and $9.95 paperback.
How to Drive an Indy Race Car
How to Fly a 747
How to Fly the Space Shuttle

Rainbow Warrior Artists Series
Each is 48 pages and $14.95 hardcover.
Native Artists of Africa
Native Artists of Europe
Native Artists of North America

Rough and Ready Series
Each is 48 pages and $12.95 hardcover.
Rough and Ready Cowboys
Rough and Ready Homesteaders
Rough and Ready Loggers
Rough and Ready Outlaws and Lawmen
Rough and Ready Prospectors
Rough and Ready Railroaders

X-ray Vision Series
Each is 48 pages and $9.95 paperback.
Looking Inside the Brain
Looking Inside Cartoon Animation
Looking Inside Caves and Caverns
Looking Inside Sports Aerodynamics
Looking Inside Sunken Treasures
Looking Inside Telescopes and the Night Sky

Ordering Information
Please check your local bookstore for our books, or call **1-800-888-7504** to order direct. All orders are shipped via UPS; see chart below to calculate your shipping charge for U.S. destinations. **No post office boxes please; we must have a street address to ensure delivery**. If the book you request is not available, we will hold your check until we can ship it. Foreign orders will be shipped surface rate unless otherwise requested;

please enclose $3 for the first item and $1 for each additional item.

For U.S. Orders

Totaling	Add
Up to $15.00	$4.25
$15.01 to $45.00	$5.25
$45.01 to $75.00	$6.25
$75.01 or more	$7.25

Methods of Payment
Check, money order, American Express, MasterCard, or Visa. We cannot be responsible for cash sent through the mail. For credit card orders, include your card number, expiration date, and your signature, or call **1-800-888-7504**. American Express card orders can only be shipped to billing address of cardholder. Sorry, no C.O.D.'s. Residents of sunny New Mexico, add 6.25% tax to total.

Address all orders and inquiries to:
John Muir Publications
P.O. Box 613
Santa Fe, NM 87504
(505) 982-4078
(800) 888-7504